Recliner Row

One woman's
journey
with cancer.

Lori Ernst

Recliner's Row by Lori Ernst
Illustrations by Gene Ernst
For ancillary rights information: Lori Ernst: glernst@mchsi.com
info@heritagebuilderspublishing.com

FIRST EDITION 2018

Contributing Editor, Dayana Martinez
Cover & Book Design, Rae Ella House
Published by Heritage Builders Publishing

HERITAGE BUILDERS
PUBLISHING

RIO VISTA, CALIFORNIA; TROY, ALABAMA; MANAGUA, NICARAGUA
HeritageBuildersPublishing.com
1-888-898-9563

ISBN 978-1-94260389-4
Printed and bound in the United States of America

FOREWORD

Little did I know that our lives would be impacted for the next forty years (and continuing) by a young couple who entered our church in Winnipeg, Manitoba. They were so "california" with a flair for fashion (Gene in a Gray knit suit with a ladybug on his lapel) and Lori with a smile that was contagious.

Little did I know that this couple would remain dear friends even after our paths continued in an unusual way. Gene and Lori arrived from CA and ultimately moved from Winnipeg to Minneapolis while Rick (my husband) and I moved from Minneapolis to Winnipeg and then to California. Somehow we managed to visit Nantucket, enjoy the color of leaves in the east and sing "Country Road, take me home...." under a giant tree in Hawaii. But most of all little did we know how precious that friendship would be through wonderfully exciting events as well as through difficult times. How often did the phone ring with Lori checking in! I along with many others, always knew Lori was available to arrive at our door from many miles away when she sensed the phone was not enough.

Little did I know that as Lori faced the trauma of cancer, she would invite us in to share the experience in such an intimate and revealing way. I am able to see the chairs standing at attention as she reported for chemotherapy. I can reach out and almost touch the strands of hair that collected everywhere but on her head. I joined her on the nights on the couch as sleep eluded her and she reached for her yellow pad to record her thoughts to share with you and me. And yes, I received her strength as I, too, faced cancer.

Thank you Lori for your willingness to embrace each of us.

Little did we know . . .

Linda Y

CHAPTER ONE

WARM BLANKET

Two weeks ago when I was in for my second biopsy, I had this nurse. She was a lovely person, one of the nicest I have met over the past month. She asked me if I wanted a warm blanket. No, I did not want a warm blanket, because I wasn't cold. So she did not give me a warm blanket. Later, she took my hand and held it the entire time during the biopsy. I did not want her to hold my hand, but she didn't ask me, so I let her hold my hand. It wasn't what I wanted, but it was what she thought I wanted or what she needed. It would have been embarrassing to try to remove my hand from her hand, so that is why I let her hold my hand.

I related this story to my daughter, and she did not want a warm blanket. She definitely didn't want her hand held. The next day my daughter told the story to a fellow pharmacist, Donna. Donna wanted both the warm blanket, and she wanted someone to hold her hand. I told still another friend the story, and he wanted the warm blanket, but no, he didn't want a stranger to hold his hand.

In this world there are any number of answers, and there is an answer for each person. There is no one right answer. That is why it is so difficult to know what to do, because sometimes we choose to do something because this is what we would want. We may assume the other person would want that too. It is important to ask and then respond accordingly.

I am sure I have erred many times doing the thing I thought someone wanted, but they did not want it at all. I am sorry for that. I suppose I am saying all this because I am learning to ask before proceeding.

CHAPTER TWO

WALKING SHOES

This is a journey and I am asked to put on my walking shoes, lace them up, begin, and then continue the journey. The good news is I don't embark on the journey alone. My family, my friends and my God have accompanied me. The decisions to be made are enormous and I have no experience, little information, and sometimes the information is incorrect or inadequate. It is my decision to make, no matter how difficult. The decision needs to be made. It matters not whether the shoe fits. I must walk even if the shoe pinches my feet or causes a blister. The path has not been smooth, but filled with ruts, and it has not been straight, but crooked —— none the less, it continues. My faith has kept me strong when I am weak and weepy. My family and friends have been ever near.

It was a Wednesday, and I was on a high and ready to go home from the hospital after my second surgery which was a mastectomy. The initial surgery was a lumpectomy. I was feeling great, but minutes before I was to leave, the surgeon made her visit. There was good news. She was pleased with the surgery and she thought the outward results were beautiful. Right? I could see nothing beautiful about my new look. Tears welled in my eyes. Time may change that perspective. The bad news after further testing was there were two single cells of cancer in the lymph nodes. Oh no! She says it matters little in further treatment, but I couldn't have felt more devastated. Home I went with much to think about and contemplate. Everyone has their own way of dealing with this kind of information. Mine is to insulate myself surrounded only by my thoughts and my faith. I am sure I have hurt and disappointed many as I continue to work through this process. I am sorry if any of you have felt left out. That was Wednesday.

Yesterday was Thursday, and the waiting continued for the pathology report. I put on my hot pink walking shoes, went out into the sunshine and the beautiful day to appreciate and breathe fully of creation. The waiting is the worst. I was ready for some good news. The sun was a welcome sight to a sometimes dark day. The surgeon called, and the news was good in that they found no other cancer in the breast. Now, I second guess my decision to do the mastectomy, but I am confident there is a reason even if I don't know what it is today. I am scheduled to meet with the medical oncologist next week to map out a plan for what happens from this point on. Each week for seven weeks there has been a major event to mark the week, and there has always been enough strength and confidence to muster through. That has been a gift.

Today, it is Friday. I continue the journey in some manner with dear ones by my side and for this I am grateful. Next week, it is Thanksgiving. There is much to be thankful for this day. As I gather with family and friends, I will hold them a little closer, love them a little more, cherish their individualities, set aside any past hurt or disappointment and be thankful.

It is time to go to the closet, put on my Nike walking shoes, and see where the path takes me today. It is too early for the sun to shine, but it is a good day. It is the day to be enjoyed. I am thankful for caring and sharing hands

CHAPTER THREE

TEN TRUMPETER SWANS

I must thank family and friends for your caring, sharing, and concern shown in so many ways. I am filled with a grateful heart. The tests, biopsies, surgeries, more tests, port implant and meeting with the oncologist to set up a plan are over. I have only to meet with the cardiologist next week, and begin chemotherapy on Thursday. It is set for once a week for 12 weeks and then once every 3 weeks for the remainder of the year, if all goes as planned. As you continue to pray. . . . . pray that I will tolerate the drugs with few side effects, and that I keep my spirits high. It has been a roller coaster ride with plans and information changing as more results have become available. I would be less than truthful if I said I took it all in stride immediately. There is much to be thankful for in this journey. I seem to have weathered the surgeries with little pain to slow me down. My faith has kept me strong and at peace, and my family and friends have been near to bolster me up when I was sinking in the mire. I have emerged with a few good laughs and some great stories to tell. I will have learned more about myself, my family and my friends that would be impossible to grasp without going through this process. Did

I choose the path? No, but I must take it, hopefully with head held high and shoes smacking the ground as I walk.

A couple of weeks ago a dear friend called me. She and her husband were at their cabin, and she was sitting on the dock when 10 beautiful, magnificent, white trumpeter swans came sweeping in and landed in the water by their dock. It had never happened before. She had been thinking about me, and she felt it was a sign that I was going to weather this storm with my head held gracefully high like the trumpeter swans. That call was an encouragement to me. Now, what a beautiful image to grasp and call to mind again and again. For this thought, your love, your hugs, your phone calls, your cards, your e-mails, your flowers, your books, your tapes.......each of these has come at a time I most needed it ,and that is not a coincidence. I CHERISH each of you in my life, and it is good. It is almost Christmas. Reach out and gather all those you love close to you, and bask in the warm and tender feelings that are bound to fill your heart and soul. I will never forget the image of the 10 trumpeter swans.

CHAPTER FOUR

JOURNEY NOTES

I am writing this in the middle of the night , because I can not sleep. I flipped on the lights of the beautifully decorated Christmas tree, turned on some soothing music, and here goes. What began as a seemingly simple journey morphed into this complex diagnostic nightmare. More doctors, nurses, technicians, support staff, and volunteers have probed, squeezed, questioned, biopsied, and performed multiple surgical procedures than I would have ever imagined. Most names are a blur, but what is remembered is a comforting word, competent completion of the task, too syrupy attempted conversation, lack of compassion or indifference, a warm touch, a smile, a concerned look, or a connection. All impact the mind, body, and spirit. During this process that started the end of September, I have been amazed by so many things: the difficult decision making process with little information or incorrect information and no help, the roller coaster of emotions when things kept changing every week, the supportive loving caring hands of family, friends and strangers, and my needs being met at the appropriate time. I have known but learned anew the value of faith, the value of close knit and caring family, the value of true and loyal friends, the value of a positive attitude, and the value of living a life surrounded by love and beauty. Previously I was aware of the impact people had on my life, but now it is amplified to being amazing and profound.

Today Thursday Dec. 13, I have started the infusion part of this long and complicated journey. By my side more doctors, nurses, technicians, volunteers, family and friends will help me navigate this year-long process. I begin with infusion every week for 12 weeks, and then switch to every third week providing my blood counts are good for the remainder of the year. I prayed and asked for the simple desires of my heart...Granted. I have prayed for guidance in the decision making...Granted. I have prayed for strength...Granted.

The first infusion day lasted 5 ½ hours. All went as planned, and I had no side effects or nausea. That is a blessing. My husband drove me to the appointment at 8:00 AM, stayed long enough to meet with the oncologist, and then off to work for him. My daughter picked me up at 1:30 PM, and we were off to Mall of America to do some Christmas shopping. I feel totally normal and have the same energy as before.

Today, during my infusion
I needed the warm blanket.
There is a time and place for
everything.

Many have had an
amazing impact on my journey.
These are the life lines that have
lifted me up and that has made
all the difference. I continue
the journey with head
held high like the graceful
trumpeter swan.

WHAT IF
i DON'T
WANT TO
PUT MY
big girl panties
ON?

CHAPTER FIVE

ALL IS NOT SUNSHINE/ BIG GIRL PANTIES

I woke up Saturday morning with a heavy heart and sadness as an overwhelming presence. It had descended upon me and caught me unaware. Even my usual Pollyanna thinking couldn't shake or push the cloud away. To alleviate any possibility of this overtaking my life, I wanted to explore the source.

Hours before I heard from a dear friend that her husband was diagnosed with spindle cell sarcoma, and they were to begin a journey similar to mine experiencing shock and venturing into the unknown. My heart ached for them. Being positive and surrounding myself with positive people has always been something to which I have been keenly aware. Now, when I am in a vulnerable compromised state, I am reminded anew of the importance of being earnest in my quest for the positive. Oh, don't worry I am not a "hide your head in the sand" type. I've read the painfully long list of possible side effects and contemplated their possible invasion into my every day life, but I will not accept any of them unless they are mine to bear and endure. So friend, don't feel the need to prepare me for my journey ahead. Just walk with me where I am at the moment, and find ways to add laughter in a sometimes gloomy day. Share with me your struggles, because I still want to be a light in your world.

After hours of verbalizing my frustration, I was ready with needing to deal with insignificant details that need to be managed by putting one foot in front of the other and continuing on the path of getting ready for Christmas, doing mundane grocery shopping, buying beautiful soft alpaca yarn for knitting to occupy my hands during infusion and ultimately finding strength in my faith. How thankful I am being enveloped by an understanding, loving, and caring husband who could just as well shake his head and walk away. Finally, I was able to silence the sadness. I put on my "happy legs" as I returned a phone call to my "10 beautiful graceful trumpeter swan" friend. She listened as I shared my crawl from the deep hole being grateful I had once again found my "happy legs". She told me to get up, pick up, and put on my BIG GIRL PANTS. It was my first laughter of the day, and I welcomed it with open arms.

The cloud had lifted and although the sun wasn't shining in my outside world, it warmed my heart and soul. My path was set straight again. I was able to venture into some state of normalcy with mouth watering pizza, the comfort of a crackling fire, a good movie, and eventually drifting into an uncomplicated sleep. I vow to keep my BIG GIRL PANTS close at hand, in plain view, and ready to be seized and used instead of being hidden and locked away in my closet. There are lessons to be learned and may I be open, and realize " All is not Sunshine". I hold in my hand a smooth white rock sent to me by a friend with these words. " For I know the plans I have for you, plans to give you hope and a future." Jeremiah 29:11 This gives me comfort and most of all hope.

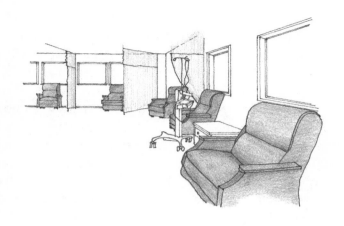

CHAPTER SIX

RECLINER ROW

Eight drab beige colored faux leather recliners with cold steel infusion poles stand at attention anxiously and patiently awaiting the arrival of the occupants for their assigned hours of daily or weekly drips. At any given moment the occupant of each chair represents a story, a life, a family, a precious loved one, a struggle, a heartache, a dream shattered, a body wracked with pain and havoc, a hard fight to be waged and hopefully won, cancer cells to be located and rendered helpless and destroyed, a spirit broken, and a hope for the future. Out of shock and sometimes despair, one needs to reach deep into the depth of one's soul and be a strong fighter, a survivor, a conqueror of that enemy that has invaded a once healthy body. All the positive experiences, all the love gathered and held tightly, all the accumulated kind words of a lifetime, all the promises of scripture are the life lines to be called upon in this arduous fight. Past hurts and negative experiences must be pushed aside and declared mute if the whole self is to be at its best to endure the fight with joy, hope and grace.

Somehow, I must reach beyond myself into the emptiness of the three to four feet that separate one fighter from another, one chair from another, perhaps with a smile, a comforting word of encouragement, a shared struggle, an outstretched hand, a nod of recognition, a quiet contented spirit, a lesson to be learned, and an experience to be cherished and shared.

Fighters must gather around to provide an amour of protection whether it be a positive attitude, positive supportive family and friends, a strong body, a deep seated faith, a joyful countenance , and a grateful heart. These are the prepared warriors to charge the enemy and fight the battle with the best assault weapons available. So many are my warriors, my soldiers, my support team, my commanders, without which I would be ill prepared to fight the battle. Regardless of the circumstances, the fight is for each of us in our own special individual ways.

Tomorrow another week has come, and I will again face the row of eight recliners and individuals assigned to each of them. It is round number two of the first set of weekly twelve rounds. I walked away from the last treatment feeling no different than when I began with relatively no side effects and for that I am amazingly thankful. Should I be surprised?

CHAPTER SEVEN

CLINICALLY SPEAKING

It's a cold blustery day, and my husband drops me off in Chanhassen to meet a friend who will drive me to treatment today. To Galleria Starbucks we go for comforting hot drinks, blueberry cinnamon scones, and a special time of connecting and sharing before she delivers me with mere minutes to spare at the Physician's Building for #2 of 12 weekly appointments at Recliner Row. Now there are nine beige recliners around the perimeter of the room. At 10:30 there is little choice of places to sit. I choose the one at the end where there is less noise, less distraction, and some artwork gracing the walls. I will have a bird's eye view of the entire room. Each chair is equipped with a side tray and I have chosen to bring a cute knitted brown snowman with red hat, scarf, and twig arms named Cornish to honor the giver and to add some funky fun to an otherwise dull impersonal space. As I settle in, I observe only one familiar face from last week. It is the cream colored hat woman and her husband. I had overheard their conversation where the husband was trying to encourage his not so willing-to-be-convinced wife that having a port installed was a good thing. Do I cross the empty barrier that separates us? Being the one week veteran of having a port installed, I decided that maybe some encouragement from me would possibly be appropriate. A brief encounter was had, and I showed the port hole protector I had made for myself to keep an extremely tender sensitive area protected from any form of rubbing. I offered my opinion on the ease of treatment with a port. They listened.

The procedure this week is the same: saline hook up, blood draw, meet with the oncologist, meet with the assistant, plastic bags of Herceptin, steroid, acid reducer, anti-allergy, and Taxol each wanting their own private time to drip into my port, veins, and body and more saline solution to finish the many drip bags of the day at 2:30. That's the clinical.

It is now one week later. I notice (one notices a lot) the previously recognized couple is getting ready to leave. Last night I had decided to make a second port hole protector in case I encountered the cream colored knitted hat woman again. I grabbed my portable cold steel infusion pole, my port hole protector, and hurried to the opposite end of the room. With few words exchanged, I showed her the device I had made for her and asked her if she wanted it. Yes, but how do I use it? I offered to put it on for her, and so begins a more personal connection with a would-be-stranger. I'm sure she is not in my path by accident. Her comment, "I was hoping I would see you today". I smiled, wished her a Merry Christmas, and went back to my chair. It took her several minutes to ready herself to leave, but instead of leaving by the door closest to her chair, she took her walker and with her husband in close pursuit, walked slowly but steadily to my end of the room. "What is your name?". she asked. We exchanged names, and other insignificant details, and the cream colored knitted hat woman became Carol as she left for the day. I will await my next prompting to reach out, to do what I can, to encounter, to smile, to connect to strangers in a sometimes cold, too busy, too many things to do, and impersonal world.

I am finished with my stint for the day. I feel normal (some may think otherwise) and after week 2 have felt no ill effects from the treatment . It is time to stuff Cornish (as it happens he has had several visitors today who appreciated his happy presence) in my black bag, put on my black coat, and hurry to the elevator to be gone from this place and to be met by my daughter at the curb with "Your limo is here" and off we go to continue Christmas shopping with oldest grandson, at Southdale for the remainder of the afternoon. He gives me a safe half hug greeting and we have things to do, places to go, things to accomplish and it is a good day.

CHAPTER EIGHT

DEVELOPING PATTERN

Somewhere between session # 2 and soon to be session # 3 a pattern has developed:

Thursday afternoon, evening, and Friday I find I am high on steroids with boundless energy and focus. I can accomplish wonders. Friday afternoon I have heated, flushed, rosy cheeks.

For a couple of weeks Saturday was a downer, but this last week was just a regular day.

The side effects are beginning to accumulate. Finally I had to admit to my husband that on Saturday irritation is very close to the surface. The warning to him helps him prepare and it is a tension breaker for us with a laugh thrown in now and then.

SUNDAY, DEC. 23

Urgent Care: Diagnosed UTI, antibiotics prescribed but within a couple of hours I know they are not working.

MONDAY, DEC. 24

Lower back pain. Ibuprofen works to some degree.

TUESDAY, DEC. 25

New antibiotics for UTI, so relief in sight. Sensitive mouth, so nothing hot, nothing spicy, nothing bubbly, or nothing tasty. The Miracle Mouth Wash helps.

√ Fingernails brittle and cracked, so no more lovely manicured nails.
√ Dry red flaky patches on face, but moisturizers help.
√ Butt rash from the toxic medicines coursing through my body.
√ Many blond hairs are appearing on the shoulders of my cashmere sweater.

But these are small matters in the relative complex present scheme of my life. I will acknowledge them, deal with them and then move forward the best way possible, being thankful that I have no nausea and generally I feel great.

Somewhere between Urgent Care and UTI relief, Christmas happened with the regular family celebrations: Our son's family of eight soon to be nine arrived for pizza on Christmas Eve; our daughter's family arrived much later for homemade ice cream and goodies; Santa arriving with a flurry of activity and, as a result, a surprise delivery is made to a chosen family in need. Beds and cots and sofas for 14 people are filled to capacity and it is well past midnight before the house once again becomes silent for a brief few hours.

Session #3 and Recliner Row is business as usual for fewer than the normal number of patients due to rescheduling for the holidays. I enter, choose the same beige recliner as last week, and settle in for the regular routine of the day. Most chairs are occupied by quiet, subdued, mostly women (a couple of men) participants who talk little, doze, sleep, never smile, and are simply just there.

Enter one fiery young redheaded tornado accompanied by an energetic blond and there is loud talk, loud laughter, phone calls to be made, the web to surf, and life to be experienced as they spend this special time together. Maybe this should be a breath of fresh air in a somewhat dismal space, but perhaps irritation is too close to the skin surface for one to appreciate the full value of the interruption. A brief amount of time passes and the fiery redhead goes into a medical crisis. Nurses fly to her aid, the privacy curtain on the far side is quickly pulled but not on my side, vitals are taken, the pharmacist appears, every available worker has come to her aid administering whatever help is needed, a volunteer brings bags of ice for her hands, and so evaporates a routine session in Recliner Row.

During this period of time the beepers from other patients needing assistance constantly beep beep calling for attention of their own, but it seems like an eternity as no one answers the calls. Later, a nurse appears, shuts off the beeping lines and returns to her post. When the crisis is over, the nurses again tend to the beeping lines.

21

Quiet and routine once again settles over Recliner Row and for this we are grateful. Christmas has passed, the body has been pumped full of fluids, the port has been flushed, the long hours have been filled, session #3 is finished, and out into crisp cold Minnesota December air I go to be reminded that "Your limo is here" as my daughter, grandson, and I go to do Christmas gift returns and exchanges. What a relief and joy to have normal tasks to complete and have the energy and the desire to do so.

CHAPTER NINE

A DAY AT RECLINER ROW

It's 2:30 AM, and it is far too early for my night of rest to be over. I've returned to the white sofa in the living room that has become my bed most nights since this journey began. I snuggle under a white cozy plush fleece blanket sent to me by my husband's sisters from Iowa to surround me and remind me with warmth of their caring, and a cream colored crocheted afghan knitted by my daughter several years ago. The sofa is a safe place to be when sleep eludes me, when I am tossing and turning in an attempt to get comfortable and back to sleep. It will not happen tonight as my brain clicks into action, and the sights, sounds, and details of my day at the infusion center fill my thoughts and I wonder will the new grandchild be born this morning. It is 3:00 AM and I surrender. I hop up and get the yellow writing pad and trusty ballpoint pen to begin to record my thoughts of session # 4.

My appointment is at 9:30 this morning so there is plenty of time to get ready. I don my black stretch pants that I have learned are necessary and easy to pull up and down as I sometimes make 5, 6, or 7 trips to the restroom with my cold steel infusion pole during the drip drip of the many bags of fluids. What goes in must go out. Another must is the white knit infusion shirt I designed and made so the nurse has easy access to my port and I have some measure of modesty in a not so private place. I add a colorful deep rose and subdued purple felted flower my husband bought for me on our recent trip to Carmel to a hot pink and black leopard animal print scarf. These add my funky touch to an otherwise ordinary outfit. Lotion is applied to my dry flaky face , hair is fluffed with far too many strands of hair accumulating in a pile on the faux white marble counter. I scarf a quick cereal breakfast while I do my daily readings and whisper a prayer for this day.

My husband and I are on our way in an off-and-on snowflake falling morning drive. We speak little as we make the 30 minute drive to the Physician's Building in Edina. Loose blond hairs flutter down like the snowflakes falling outside. I open my window a crack just enough to let them fly away, and think maybe, come spring, some bird will feather the nest with these soft hairs. The reality of the process bears down on me. I am reminded that I too will need to put on a hat, a scarf or a turban to cover my naked head. Nothing screams cancer louder than the sight of a hairless head covered in some manner. My husband drops me off, and returns to the office to work on his projects.

The faces at the reception desk have become familiar. I check in, and then wait in the lobby reading the daily news-paper until a nurse summons my name and leads me to the room I now call Recliner Row. There is only one patient in the room and I can't believe she has taken "my chair". I smile, acknowledge her, and say good choice in chairs as I walk on.

Visualize the room: facing a bank of windows the nine chairs are numbered left to right. A rather young, pale faced, blue/grey turban clad woman is sitting in chair number 9 on the right. I have many other choices, but I choose number 1 for the location next to a wall, the proximity to the restroom, and the distance from the other occupied chair. My nurse today is a trainee and her supervisor hovers over her as she begins the tedious process of taking vitals, flushing the port, inserting the special 3/4" cored right angle needle into my port and taking blood samples to be tested before the treatment can begin. For whatever reason flushing the port today is done 3 times, and it still doesn't work. The supervisor gives suggestions: lean her chair back, have her lift her arm, lean her chair back further, have her lay on her side, and have her put her arm over her head. Each is tried and finally the port is functional and the vials are filled with blood and taken for testing. Now, the pharmacist can determine my exact regimen for the day. The nurse records information into a computer as she asks question after question about how I am feeling, symptoms I may or may not have had for the week, any problems I am dealing with, what new medications I may have added, what medications need to be crossed off the list, and a myriad of other questions. It is a long and laborious process for the trainee and takes far longer than usual. I am not even hooked up to the saline solution before it is time for me to meet with the oncologist.

I am escorted beyond the room I have been in the past 3 weeks. I am relieved that I don't have to sit and stare at the picture on the wall in that former room that says, "50% of people with cancer now survive". Is that supposed to be positive? In the new room, I grab a magazine, read, and wait until there is a knock on the door, and in pops my oncologist. She is this long dark haired, dark skinned, petite, young woman who graduated from Gandhi Medical College in India. With a easy smile, a firm shake of the hand, and a greeting this quick-minded, thorough, precise, 'let's get this done' attitude woman is prepared for our appointment. We mainly talk about my week, discuss my problems, find ways to deal with them, determine I need x-rays to find the cause of my aching back, and check my lungs and heart.

A couple of weeks ago when we had finished with all our medical discussion, she had asked me some interior design questions about prints, paintings, and framing. Since that time, I had done some research for her and handed her a purple 9 ½" x 11" envelope filled with pictures and prints she could consider and a website she could browse. Although she had initiated the conversation previously, she found herself on uncommon ground. She was stunned I had taken the time and effort to try to meet a need of hers when my need was her priority. She thumbed through the pages, liked what she saw, thanked me, and was gone. I only ask that I be seen as a person with a life, a job, a family, and friends and not just another cancer patient that she sees hour by hour and day by day. Her assistant appears and works her magic at scheduling my remaining appointments

for the first 12 weeks ending in late February, if I am able to stay on course with no interruption because of low counts. One hour has passed and I am back at Recliner Row hooked up and settled in for the day.

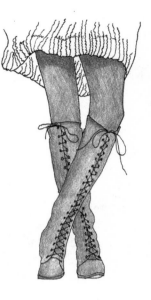

In comes a woman with short 1" long hair, stretch jeans, designer boots, big bulky sweater and a colorful scarf followed by presumed to be husband. She chooses chair number 3, sits down, pulls out a hat from her bag, puts it on, and she too is ready for her treatment. The husband takes his seat in a row of burgundy side chairs facing the recliners with some six feet separating them. He takes out his book, spends almost the entire time reading, interrupted only to share 1/2 of a courtesy provided turkey sandwich with his wife, who reads and knits to pass the time.

Next comes a masked woman in a wheelchair, pushed by a masked man, and accompanied by another masked woman who chooses chair number 5. (They are fighting respiratory issues) One on each side, they lift her up, maneuver her into the recliner, and then each take a burgundy chair from the row and pull them up close to her one on either side. They are attentive, talk quietly, and the husband tenderly holds and strokes her hand. She sits, feet up, covered by a warm blanket as she accepts her treatment.

A far-too-young woman wearing a cute lavender crocheted hat enters and chooses the private room. She is

accompanied by an equally young woman. I see no more of them as they are sequestered in that dark private place of her own choosing. The wall that separates me from the only other private space equipped with a hospital bed for the sickest of patients is now occupied by another turbaned young woman. She is not alone. A friend, a sister, or whoever takes a chair from the row and moves it close by her bed and I hear nothing from that room, but they are there.

A wiry silver gray haired older, (knows the routine) woman shuffles in the room and chooses chair number 2 next to mine. She is brusque, demanding, opinionated, and definitely keeps the nurses in line. She dozed off and on while she receives her allotment for the day from bags suspended from her steel pole.

The spaces are filling up even though four patients have called and canceled for the day because of the weather. The last person to arrive on my watch is a dark skinned, probably less than 30-year-old, woman with slicked back tight to the head jet black hair. I recognize her from last week, and she is accompanied by another young brown skinned woman and she chooses chair number 7.

As I have observed this day, I find it interesting that nary a patient acknowledges, smiles, or nods in recognition of another patient during these 4 weeks I have come to this place. My only personal contact with another patient was with the cream colored hat woman named Carol to whom I was first to initiate the conversation. My thought is next week I will attempt to see if these barriers can or should be broken to some degree. I am saddened to think that my brief encounter with Carol could be my last.

It is 1:15. The bags are empty, the port is flushed and I am ready to step outside and battle the windy, frigid cold January day as I cross the street to the hospital for the scheduled x-rays. Task completed and my daughter is there in her black Honda limo to whisk me away to Costco for grocery shopping and back to her house where my husband will pick me up and take me home.

It is 5:30. We are home and I am glad there are many options for dinner to choose from waiting in the freezer. I have planned ahead and chow mein, several soups, chicken Alfredo, chicken wings, roast beef with potatoes and carrots, lasagna, spaghetti, and potato/tomato au gratin are the available choices. My husband chooses the beef, and we eat, watch the news and relax. I am pumped with steroids so many projects get done this night. My daughter calls to remind me to take my benadryl and ibuprofen 45 minutes before I intend to sleep. My planning was not good and an hour and a half had passed before I actually went to bed. It was good enough to get me to sleep, but not good enough to keep me asleep. I have been awake since 2:30. I have spent the entire time writing, and now it is 6:45 AM. I will try again to sleep.

Eventually I do sleep and am awakened suddenly by the ringing of the phone. It is our son and he announces another granddaughter was born this morning. All is well. Joy and sadness mingle together as so often happens in this complicated convoluted world. We are excited to see this latest grandchild and do so. She is lovely, she is healthy, she is beautiful and she is welcomed into our family as I snuggle her close, marveling at the miracle of it all and I feel at peace.

It's Saturday and in a matter of two days my fluffy seemingly alive blond hairs have fallen from my head so rapidly I can scarcely believe it. What remains clings helplessly to my head. The pink plastic hair pick rakes dead disconnected strands of fine hairs from my scalp as I look in the mirror. I am stunned and shocked at their hasty departure. Tonight, we are invited out for dinner and for the first time I desperately search in my scarf drawer to discover something appropriate to cover my partially naked head. I have joined the ranks of the easily recognized cancer patient and I am emotionally unprepared for the reality of it all. Random tears trickle and streak my rosy cheeks, but this too I will conquer. The strongest soldiers must be sent to fight the most difficult battles and may be found worthy.

IT'S STILL ME
WIG STUDIO

CHAPTER TEN

GONE SHOPPING

Tuesday 2:30 AM, a familiar time and I am summoned from a peaceful sleep. Almost immediately, I know I will not soon return to slumber. A quick trip to the darkened family room to retrieve my yellow tablet and pen reminds me that the untold story nestled somewhere within my foggy brain is wanting to be told. Each word or sentence tumbles easily from brain to paper surface. I struggle to balance my need to put words to my thoughts and the appropriateness of sharing those private thoughts with others. I hate the realization that this has become an unwanted pattern of what should be the sleeping hours in my life. The cruel reality of my journey consumes more time and energy than I want willingly to allow. The dark and stillness of night fosters too many needless thoughts and concerns, and it opens me up to the vulnerability of letting my mind wander unnecessarily into that realm.

It is 4:45 AM and I am wanting for sleep. I am wanting for a stilled mind. I am wanting to drift off, and I am willing to battle to that end. Wanting and achieving can be a far distance from each other at opposite spectrums. The stomach growls, the heart pounds, and anxiety hovers close to the surface as sleep seems so desperate to elude. The stately grandmother clock refuses to be muffled into silence as it announces every quarter, every half, every-three-quarter, and every hour throughout the night. A wide chasm separates the wanting and the achieving. Finally, at seven bells I refused to be kept prisoner any longer and rise to start the day in earnest thinking *"Be joyful in hope, be patient in affliction, faithful in prayer"* **Romans 12:12.**

It has been five days since the massive hair departure began. Each morning the mirror anxiously welcomes me. The blushing pink plastic pick nestled among the other, brushes, combs and picks is waiting to perform its duty. I methodically lift and fluff the silky blond hair as literally piles of hair accumulate on the white counter top. Sadness and regret pass silently through my muddled mind.

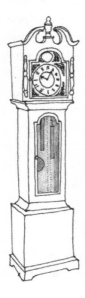

Today shall be the appointed day to venture out into the wig world and explore the possibilities. My trusty partner daughter meets me at a little strip mall and we drive to an aptly named "It's Still Me" studio in a strange looking stucco building that is larger on the top and narrower at the bottom. The short ride on the elevator deposits us on the 4th floor. Jan greets us quickly. She in in deep conversation with the UPS woman who is delivering and depositing stacks of boxes.

The consultant ushers us from the ante room to the main room approximately

10' x 14' surrounded on two sides with windows and an entire shelved wall with wigged heads of silver, blond, red, brown, black, and any shade in between staring blankly at us and waiting patiently to be chosen. It is a sunny 30 degree day and the sun streams through the window as the tall, exuberant, red haired dynamo dressed in a lace printed  short skirt, a long sleeved black t-shirt, black tights, and a huge black leather belt slung low on her hips begins with her short course of Wig 101.

The owner was a former cancer patient so she understands. Information absorbed, we begin the long and tedious process of putting wig to head to determine what color, style, and length would look most natural for me. Many are tried from the ridiculous to laughable to not so bad. As it turns out, the one just delivered by the UPS woman, and the first one tried on was the one selected. With wild lime green bag in hand and with the credit card smoking in shock, we leave this place with a visual reminder that the soon to be bald head will be covered with a fashionable, short styled, and a bit funky wig. Being made aware that this hair thing will last a year or more while I will be forced to wear this cranial prosthesis adds a heaviness to a once light hearted person. " It's Still Me".

To make it a red banner day and to add insult to injury we decide to make a rather dreaded trip to "Underneath It All" for a prosthesis of another kind. The certified fitter measures and observes my body to choose a form that closely resembles my own one remaining. Garments are tried and rejected. My trusty companion has left me on my own, because this is too personal a task to need a third opinion. Emotion again surprises me and bubbles to the surface as tear droplets steal their way from deep within. The experienced understanding fitter drapes a soft warm bed jacket over my shoulders and exits the dressing room to try again to find the perfect fit and to leave me some time alone. At some point when we are still trying another style and size the words tumble from my lips," That's terrible". She nods her head and says "You are right" and again leaves me alone so she can search for other options. It is time for me to find my big girl pants and put them on and continue the process. At last, we are successful and I am surprised by the generosity of the insurance companies to cover a large portion of these expenses. I walk out of the shop alone but not alone with pink shopping bag in hand, relieved that another milestone has passed and grateful success was achieved.

**Much has been accomplished and Session #5
is less than two days away, and I am ready.**

CHAPTER ELEVEN

WALKING THROUGH THE STORM

Arriving at Recliner Row at 8 AM, I am surprised chairs number 4, number 6, and number 8 are already occupied by three women and the remaining chairs stand at attention beckoning to me. I choose chair number 1 where bright light streams through the windows from directly behind the faux leather beige chairs. Again the trainee is my nurse and again there is a problem with the blood flow. I am quickly surrounded by 3 nurses as they pool their knowledge and experience to come up with a plan. They collectively decide to inject a medicine to open up the area. We must wait 30 minutes for it to work its magic and see if it is deemed effective.

During this interlude, my husband accompanies me as I meet with the oncologist. As she thoroughly answers each question on my list, she does her checks, and announces she'll be on vacation for a week. The meeting with the raven haired oncologist is over and I return to chair #1 and wait.

During the long wait, the blood draws are delayed, the lab testing is on hold, and nothing more can be done until we have the filled vials for testing. The medicine delivered by syringe through my port doesn't open the flow, so I suggest for the second time this day that we try the position we tried last week that had proven successful. The trainee asks which position that was because she can't remember me until she sees me out flat, on my side with hand over my head and then she remembers. We try it, and it works. I am reminded of U.S. President Theodore Roosevelt's "speak softly and carry a big stick" quote at the Minnesota State Fair Sept. 2, 1901. I've discovered one must try and try again, one must poke and poke until someone listens, one must never, never, give up and one must be an advocate for oneself. Now, the samples are taken, labeled and delivered.

At this time a woman and her husband leave abruptly. Her session is canceled because her body is unable to withstand the assault. She must go home, rest, regain her strength, and wait for her body to recover enough to return next week to continue her treatment. My wait is long and anxiety creeps into my thoughts as I contemplate the possibility of my being unable to take my treatment today. My nurse assures me the results are not yet back from the lab because there are many lab tests to be done, many formulas to make because all 9 chairs and the two private spaces are full while another patient waits patiently for someone to leave so she too may have a chair. Finally, the bags are delivered and I am relieved session #5 will be completed as planned. Later, when the lab paperwork is printed and delivered, I am told that for the second week my liver functions are elevated and an ultrasound of my abdomen is needed. It is scheduled for tomorrow to attempt to determine the cause of the elevation.

Following my plan to connect with other patients during my time here, I stop briefly and greet the lavender crocheted hat woman and the other woman who has accompanied her today. I simply smile and ask about her day. She smiles, answers my questions and not wanting to intrude too much in her space, I move quickly on.

Later, when I am up and moving about with my steel pole, I stop at the private room with the hospital bed. It is the same short dark haired woman who occupied that room last week. The man who brought her has left and she is alone reading. Our encounter is much the same as with the lavender hat young woman, and again I move on quickly. It is a start, a new beginning and I think nothing ventured, nothing gained.

I busy myself with paperwork, read a magazine, try to knit but can't concentrate, so I doze to pass the time. Five hours have passed and the bags are all empty, the port is flushed, and my session is finished.

A red Cadillac limo arrives. The driver is a friend I met years ago in high school. She picks me up, and delivers us to the posh shops of the Galleria. We will meet my goddaughter and her mother-in-law for lunch. We talked, we shared lunch, we laughed, we told stories and we enjoyed our brief time together, but there are things to do, places to go, people to see, schedules to keep, so we parted as one returns home to Buffalo, New York, one to work, and one delivers me home. Busy lives are the norm in the world today, and the words of a song I first learned in high school float through my mind.

"When you walk through a storm
Hold your head up high
and don't be afraid of the dark
At the end of the storm is a golden sky
And the sweet silver song of the lark.

Walk on through the wind
Walk on through the rain,
Though your dreams be tossed and blown

Walk on, walk on with hope in your heart
And you'll never walk alone."

———————

Author, **John Farnham**

These words bring comfort
and I know I never walk alone.

CHAPTER TWELVE

MANY HAVE WALKED
BEFORE ME

I stand surprised and utterly amazed as my parents have bolted from the confines of the grave to join with me and walk with me on this journey. I have been comforted by the unexpected memories and dreams and have felt a closeness to them unsurpassed in the years since their passing. I recall many and varied details of their own cancer journeys those many years ago when we were separated by miles and miles of roads and highways and lived in states a far distance from each other.

Within days of my marriage (years ago), my mom who had purposely waited until after the celebration to go to the doctor embarked on her own journey that resulted in a double mastectomy. She was ahead of her time in thinking and just wanted to be done with the worry of what a future diagnosis might bring, so she chose the extreme. Beyond the surgery she had no further treatment and carried the scars for 39 years with grace and dignity. I look back at it now and I am in awe.

My 91-year-old dad had his own cancer diagnosis. He had a similar regiment of treatment and had a high like mine after treatment when he was propelled forward with energy, excitement, and lifted spirit. At times that drove my mother crazy because my farmer dad wanted to go out for coffee, visit friends, and tinker with machinery. I marvel at their strength and steadfastness. That example makes my road much easier to travel. The beauty of memories and the blessing of memories continue to surround me with their presence in a time when it is so wonderfully welcomed. I am comforted by the close- ness of our relationship those many years together with no fences needing to be mended and with no bridges needing to be fixed and I can just bask in how special it was.

It has been days since my pen was silenced when someone questioned my journaling and sharing. I have bravely taken pen in hand again to continue the chronicle with deeper understanding, renewed spirit, and more dependence on my faith to shelter me from harm. For those who have accompanied me, I am filled with your presence, your love, your caring, and am uplifted.

The halfway point (session 6) has arrived and passed with the anticipated relief and gratitude for my toleration of the "dreaded" therapy. To have been spared from what I deem the worst of the possible side effects, I am exceedingly thankful. Family and friends have given me the sticks, the twigs, the reeds, the hair, and the mud to build a sturdy nest in a sheltered place away from the wind, rain, and harm.

My nest has been feathered with caring hands. I have been able to fly away and return again to the soft comfort of the nest to rest, to warm myself, to be content, to be patient, to be renewed, and to fly away again and again with strong wings to soar to heights and places unknown.

CHAPTER THIRTEEN

THE TIME OF RECKONING

The time has come and I stand poised with the electric black hair trimmer ready to embark on yet another venture. Before I have time to put clipper to my head, in walks my beloved of 50 years. He looks at me and asks if I want or need help. It is so important to ask the question. The answer is yes and he tenderly rows out the first strip from the nape of my neck to top of my head and deposits the small pile on the counter. He warns me he has no experience, but I nod to just continue because who needs experience?

He is here, and that is all that matters. The task continues until all that remains is a stubble of hair that feels weird to the touch as I run my bare hand over his handiwork. Ears that once were hidden from view become antennae protruding from my head. Movies are made with creatures like this. The good news is from now on there won't be all this long doglike hair on the maple hardwood floors gathering dust and needing to be constantly swept or vacuumed. Always, if one looks there is a bright light at the end of the tunnel.

CHAPTER FOURTEEN

FINDING THE BEAUTIFUL

Once there was a Beautiful Woman who had a dilemma.
When she looked in the mirror she had only 3 hairs.
What can I do with 3 hairs?
Oh, I have an idea, I'll braid the 3 hairs,
And she did.
She looked in the mirror and said, "Isn't that Beautiful?"

The next day the Beautiful Woman, who had a dilemma
Looked in the mirror and now she only had 2 hairs.
What can I do with only 2 hairs?
Oh, I have an idea, I'll make 2 pony tails,
And she did.
She looked in the mirror and said, "Isn't that Beautiful?"

On the third day the Beautiful Woman who had a dilemma
Looked in the mirror and discovered she had only 1 hair left.
What can I do with only 1 hair?
Oh, I have a wonderful idea, I'll make a single pony tail,
And she did.
She looked in the mirror and said, "Isn't that Beautiful?"

At last the Beautiful Woman who had a dilemma
Looked in the mirror and she had no hair.
What can I do with no hair?
Oh, I don't have to worry about my hair anymore,
"And isn't that a Beautiful thing?"

~ Story told at oncology convention, author anonymous

What we Look For, We See.

I am reminded of a couple of incidents that took place early in this arduous journey. The first surgery was behind me, but a second surgery loomed ahead. The second surgery was finished, and it was time for the post operative visit with the surgeon.

With my forever changed body that was tender and healing I arrived at the surgeon's office. You know the routine, check in at the reception desk, fill out the forms again and again, wait until called, get assigned to a room, told to strip to the waist and put on a gown opening at the front, and wait patiently until the surgeon appears. She arrives, smiles, greets me, and asks the regular routine questions. Then she says, "Let's take a look". Being the modest person that I am and a bit apprehensive when I am baring my new body for the first time, but I comply. She nonchalantly says, "it's beautiful". Words choke in my throat and tears well up in my eyes as I mumble, "That's not what I would call it". The rivulets slowly trickle down my face. I was unprepared for the emotion that rested so close to the surface of my bruised and battered body and spirit. I understood the technical beauty of the job she had done, but I could think of many other words that would not have unearthed the feelings inside.

What we Look For, We See.

Just one day after this encounter with my surgeon, I met with my oncologist for the first time. Remember, she is the dark skinned, raven haired, petite, young woman, with firm handshake and an easy smile. This is the preliminary meeting and she has reviewed my tests, wants to learn a bit about me, and meet the person she will be dealing with throughout this long and difficult journey. On paper, I am seemingly old and fragile, but after spending some time with me she quickly discovers I am not fragile. When did I become old? Inside my brain, I am still young and vibrant, but the years have played a dirty trick on me, and the numbers do not lie. If I were both old and fragile, one option would be to have no further treatment. She wants to confer with her colleagues to determine what treatment would be most appropriate and beneficial for me.

Again, I have been asked to strip to the waist, and have covered myself with one of those muted grey/mauve gowns. She wants to have a look. The first words out of her mouth are, "It is beautiful". You would think I would be prepared, but I am not. Again, my voice quivers, tears well up, and I say, " Those wouldn't be the words I would use." I am stunned that two days in a row, both my surgeon and my oncologist, who are both women, have used the same words to describe my incision. She apologizes and quickly exits the room. Alone, I have a chance to regain my composure and mentally prepare for her return grappling with the challenge of it all. She returns and profusely apologizes and says she has learned something very important from me this day, and she will not make that mistake again. In that moment she understood where I was coming from emotionally and saw not just the handiwork of the surgeon, but me as a person. Twelve weeks down the road from this incident, I would be less affected emotionally by the same words, but I would still not want to hear those words. Maybe, something like "good job "or "fine job" would be more palatable words for me to hear.

Beauty is in the Eyes of the Beholder.

I've always been attracted to and influenced by beautiful things whether it is the dazzling sunset, glittering diamonds, sparkling ocean, perfectly formed lovely flowers, surprise of a simple rainbow, myriad coloring of the feathers of a bird, shiny silver and gold baubles, beauty of a snowfall, spectrum of fabulous colors, fabric with a soft hand, fine cut of a garment, or the artsy use of materials. My eyes see, my spirit soars, and my creativity expands while observing and experiencing these things. Travel has become a way to observe anew, to shop, to explore, and to be, where things are new and different and time is of little importance. I am able to drink it all in, savor the beauty of it all, and add it to the storehouse to be recalled when life needs a special boost.

What we Look For, we See.
What we Touch, we Feel.
What we Search For, we Find.

These are beautiful things, but people are beautiful in their own right. Although we gaze, admire and emulate the features that seem to make up the beautiful, the outward appearance is far less important to me than the beauty that is within. The outward will change and fade over time, but what lies inside has the possibility of being enhanced, perfected, fine tuned with deeper understanding, skills, compassion, and love. It is almost impossible to separate the outward and the inner beauty of those we love, care for, and observe from a distance, but it is the sum total that melds together and we remember.

> *"What lies behind us, and what lies before us, are tiny matters compared to what lies within us"*
>
> ~ Emerson

I have been drawn to beautiful places again and again. I experience intrigue and excitement in discovering the new and different. There is comfort in the familiar sought after places that enrich our lives, comfort our souls, renew our spirits, and settle our hurried days. I find pleasure in rugged snow covered mountains, walks in alpine meadows with tiny perfect flora, but equally pleasurable are the bubbling creek, roaring river, or swelling ocean. Sitting beside the vast ocean and feeling the cool breeze brush my cheeks as the waves rise and crash on the sun drenched sand is a way of finding the beautiful in nature. Along with these God created places, man has added his own touch to the beautiful landscape whether here or abroad. There are the phenomenal intricacies of the Eiffel Tower, magnificent cathedrals of Europe, ruins of the Coliseum, Golden Gate Bridge in San Francisco, welcoming torch of the Statue of Liberty, Big Ben, and countless other symbols. Each has touched and enriched my life in profound ways.

*"Though we travel the world over to find the
beautiful, we must carry it with us or we find it not."*

~ Emerson

Once there was a woman who had a dilemma,
she was faced with 9 ugly faux leather chairs at what became
known as Recliner Row. What should I do with ugly chairs?
Oh, I have an idea. These chairs have welcomed
people with needs, people with names, people
with lives, and people with loved ones, so I must
look at them more closely. Over time these chairs
have become familiar, comfortable, encompassing,
necessary, and even somewhat inviting. Could it be
that these chairs too are beautiful in their own way?

A small wicker basket filled to overflowing with
knited hats and wrist warmers, turbans, visors, and caps
has been placed on the counter in Recliner Row by caring
and loving hands. Once this basket and its contents invaded
my thoughts, and I deemed it unpleasant. I have
since walked up to that small basket, and chosen a
hat carefully that was lovingly knitted by a stranger and
in the process found the beautiful.

What we look for we see.

Patients:
Please
help
your self!!

CHAPTER FIFTEEN

FINDING FRIENDSHIP

Nine Thursdays have come and gone and this morning it is number 10. My little old driver so lively and quick, hustles us out the door early, because we have been warned the roads are icy in spots, slushy, or snow packed in other areas and the traffic has backed up for miles with spin outs scattered along the way. We arrive late and I hurry with my black purse and my black bag slung over my shoulder brimming with projects to the 6th floor where the elevator deposits me at the reception desk. The lobby chairs are all empty, and no one is waiting to check in. I flash my prettily decorated personal laminated card. It contains the answers to the questions they ask each time I check in: name, birthdate, have you fallen, and are you safe in your home. It still gets a smile or a chuckle. With my identification tag on my wrist, I am told to make my own way to the back room. The nurse smiles as she opens the door, ushers me in, and I discover I am the first patient to arrive. I am a creature of habit, so for 8 of the 10 sessions I choose chair number 1 and it welcomes me home with the early morning sun streaming through the east facing windows. There are anywhere from 6-8 women workers manning their stations. The roving pharmacist, Marty, passes through at intervals throughout the day talking to his patients as he delivers the drugs from some unknown place in the building.

After a short time other patients begin to arrive, and the lavender/rose knitted hat woman sequesters herself in the private room as she has done every week. A new man moves slowly and deliberately with his shiny metal walker to the other private room, because he says he must lie down. The curtain is pulled and little is heard from that space, and long before I am finished, he is gone, the bed stripped, ready, and waiting. Today, for only the third time, I see the funky short haired woman with leather laced fashion boots and black leggings come in to claim her regular chair. At this point she and I are the only occupants of Recliner Row. As before, her husband takes his seat in a burgundy chair opposite the beige chairs and pulls out his paperback book and begins to read.

Friends come into our lives, for a reason, for a season, or for a lifetime. Throughout life one meets, and connects, or not, and both parties determine where it will go from there. For us to connect we must be on the same page at the same time needing a relationship. We can find examples of friendship from childhood playmates, high school peers, college acquaintances, work affiliates, neighbors, church congregants, and endless other possibilities. As I look back and forward, I can see examples of friendship for a reason, a season, and a lifetime. Before I was aware of this concept I thought a friendship was a failure, if it was not maintained no matter how fragile, unhealthy, or unnecessary the relationship. I am determined to put myself out there, be open, be observant, and be available. From the beginning I have wanted to use this experience to reach out to the people who have been placed in my life as we share a similar journey.

Back in my chair, I pick up my #13 bamboo knitting needles, candy pink yarn, hot pink yarn, and rose colored yarn to knit a headband for one of my twin granddaughters. While I am knitting, the leather laced fashion boot woman and her husband walk toward me. She smiles, says hi, and they exit to meet with the doctor. After about 30 minutes they return, she stops to inquire about my knitting (she crochets), asks for the pattern, but the nurse is trying desperately to hurry her on. I proceed to write down the pattern and the nurse says she'll copy it. I promise to explain the directions to fashion boot woman later when she settles in. Just before she surrenders to the nurse, she leans over close and whispers, "Do you have breast cancer too?" I nod and she returns to her faux leather recliner.

At Recliner Row my early encounter with the beige knitted hat woman who became Carol lasted but two sessions. I had hoped and prayed that we would meet again, but so

far that has not happened. It was impossible at first to think that the possibility of a deeper friendship was all but over and she was in my life and I was in her life only for a brief moment or two. To believe there was still value in that brief encounter that I have been rendered helpless to change, but I smile, I find joy, I fondly remember, and I cherish the fleeting exchange. To have walked toward her, to have linked our lives, to have offered to share, to have entered her private space was my own part, but she too walked toward me, entered my space, linked with me, and accepted my outstretched hand. That was enough for both of us to be noticed, to feel cared for, to lighten the load, and to be filled up for each of us to continue our own journey with purpose and determination. I have discovered again that perseverance, awareness, and patience have led me thus far in facing the inevitable, and these people are not mere chance encounters in life.

On one of my trips up and about, I pass the private room and we both nod and smile at one another. These are the only chances to greet, because at other times, she has company, the nurse is there, she is sleeping, and then she is gone before I leave for the day. My knitting is finished, but more important my plastic bags hung from the steel pole are empty, and I am dismissed for the day.

Before putting on my black down filled coat, I walk over to chair number 4 to keep my promise and show her the finished headband. We talked first about our yarn projects, our yarn supply (mine from when my friend and I owned and operated Heartland Knits and hers from buying out all the yarn from a going-out-of-business yarn shop in nearby Excelsior). Our conversation progressed seamlessly into our cancers and treatment, our work (we both worked at downtown Dayton's), our families, where we lived, and did I have a husband. Finally she asked if I had a card with my name and number, and did I want to get together for dinner with the four of us? This exchange of information occurred in a mere 15-20 minutes and was a brief encounter of another kind because we had bonded on many levels. Where it goes from here is a mystery and dependent on one of us making the first move to branch out to a place other than infusion row. I have her number and her name.

Although I have talked to the infusion pharmacist many times previously, last week I had asked him if my grandson who is a second year pre-pharmacy student could shadow him to learn about a different aspect of the profession. He was most gracious and agreed to do it. We settled on a day when my grandson would be home on spring break, and he gave me his calling card. I gave my pharmacist daughter the card, and she dug deep in her memory bank and maybe her closet and discovered she had graduated with Marty. A fellow worker at her place of employment knew him too since she also was at University of Minnesota. What a small world. Fast forward to this week and Marty is delivering drugs. I wave him over and relayed the previous information to him. His eyes opened wide, he grinned, he knew my name, and immediately connected the dots and said my daughter's name. He couldn't believe that he could pull her name out after 30 years. We talked briefly and he continued with his work. After the initial shock, he returned again and again for long conversations to piece together the puzzle of all the people we knew in common and marveled at the unexpected connected trail in our lives.

Today is Valentine's Day and every one seems in a celebratory spirit or happy mood, or was it because over time we have become more familiar and open? Maybe it was some of both. When my husband dropped me off this morning he gave me a small black box tied with a red ribbon and an oil on canvas red heart mounted on the top. He said it was a surprise for me to open during my session. Inside was a message of our conversation from the very first day we drove to begin my treatment. In part it read, "On the first day of Chemo, my true love gave to me , his heart in a Caring Tree". He had decided he would paint a miniature oil painting for each of my 12 chemo days the first being a picture of his office with a red heart hanging in the tree outside. His idea changed over time, he did paint the tree with the heart, but changed and painted the 12 days of Christmas. What a treasure. The details are incredible from my crazy artsy loving husband. I exited Recliner Row with a spring in my step, a smile on my face, energy to burn, and stories to relate to family and friends retelling the wonder of it all.

Be open, be friendly, be available, and a path becomes clear. Where it leads is a mystery, but it matters not whether we meet people for a reason, a season, or a lifetime.

The lifetime friendships gathered, nurtured, rekindled, and cherished over these many years are the very people who have wanted to share this journey with me. We have so many collective shared memories: of family, friends, trips, cruises, movies, concerts, gourmet dinners, a picnic in the park, books, events, a simple meal, ideas, political opinions, religious differences, joy of birth, sadness of death and illness, of struggles and heartache. They all meld together in one rich tapestry that sustains me. All have brought us closer together in the sharing. "The Five Love Languages" by Gary Chapman that I taught to the African women on a mission trip to Mozambique was a wonderful lesson. A reminder that we all have different ways to express our love and it becomes our love language of choice. According to Chapman whether one chooses words of affirmation, quality time, gifts, acts of service, or physical touch to express love, it is important that the receiver knows it is a love language and values it as such. Finding friendship and placing a gold, silver, or diamond value to it endures the gift like the precious metals and jewels that they are.

The sleepless nights in Victoria have been fewer, shorter, and farther between; hence, there are fewer and wider spaced writings. I have found I have greater appreciation for writers and their books. It takes far more time than I would have ever imagined to draft these small chronicles. I appreciate your love languages whatever the method and feel a bond to you in a far different way than before.

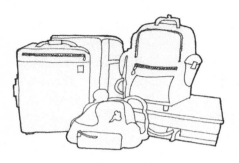

CHAPTER SIXTEEN

THE LUGGAGE WE CARRY/ THE BAGGAGE WE CARRY

A few weeks ago, I had called a friend who had lost her husband a year ago and we were having a conversation about loss and the loads we each must carry. She told the story of the night she and her husband were lying in bed side by side after learning of the devastating news about his illness. As they were talking through the difficulty of accepting the diagnosis, she asked him whom he would like to give his burden to. After a weighty silence, there was no one, no family member, no friend, absolutely NO ONE and then they knew they must carry it themselves. As she and I talked, we were aware that each one of us has one sort of baggage that we must carry. How then can we carry it without stooped shoulders, without feeling sorry for ourselves, without bitterness, but with grace and dignity?

There is no reason our bag has to be big, heavy, or ugly. A little glitter or sparkly, a pretty scarf or ribbon, a meaningful talisman, or any other fun embellishment can make an otherwise ordinary bag pretty or personal.

At some point or several times throughout our lifespan, we have found ourselves shopping for luggage. The brand names are endless and the choices monumental. Walk or stroll through any luggage department and the array of options are overwhelming. Whether we choose American Tourister, Hartmann, Amelia Earhart, Tumi, Eagle Creek, Louis Vuitton, Kipling, Travel Pro, or any other name or nameless brand, we will find what we so desperately are searching for to meet our needs. This is the luggage we carry.

From the screaming infant who is welcomed, hoped for, prayed for, or the baby who arrived unplanned, unwanted, and uncared for, people have impacted each life. Some have been lovingly nurtured, and others abused or neglected, or others still tolerated or ignored. Whatever the circumstances of the birth or the impact of playmates, peers, teachers, acquaintances, friends, fellow workers, or even the sales clerk at the local supermarket, these people have made a difference in how we see ourselves today. All have left an indelible handprint on who we have become. The beautiful child is treated differently than the plain or handicapped; the brightest student in class is treated differently than the slow learner; the biggest star on the sports team from the struggling athlete; the fastest runner from the methodical plodder; the talented musician from the plunk plunk piano player; the fast track executive from the office help; the skillful speaker from the stagehand; and the list goes on. Each of these encounters we have brushed against have left a profound mark on our lives in either positive or negative ways and this is the baggage we carry. Most often this is talked about in a negative way, but I want to consider it in a positive manner.

In packing for our travel journey, a list is an important tool to use to check off the essentials. The day of taking a bag as big as possible and as many bags as wanted seem to have changed with the extra charges for overweight or oversized luggage that the airlines are now so often charging. The airlines are driving our luggage use and teaching us a new way to travel. Why not transfer this to our life journey.

What size bag are we willing and able to carry with ease? With the list in hand, we start to accumulate the items we will need. Sometimes with little thought we dream, we stack our things, and we hang in a special spot the possible items we wish to consider. How many shirts do I need? How many trousers? Do I need a hat? How many and what kind of shoes? Yes, yes, check, check off all those essentials. As the time gets closer we make final decisions, we pare down, and we eliminate as many things as we are willing to part with for this trip. Likewise, in life the assembly line of choices is enormous. Through this life we've had hurts, heartaches, experiences, circumstances, accidents, and other "stuff" we are just dealt. Whether it is luggage or baggage we choose to carry it, abandon and discard what you do not need and replace it with something much easier to carry.

First, I choose to carry only one piece of luggage with wheels, because it is easier to maneuver and almost effortless to pull. I want a sturdy handle long enough to be able to piggyback my purse, coat, and a small backpack if necessary. As I watch the assembly line of life pass by it is easier for me to let anger, resentment, and jealousy pass by. It is more difficult for me to let hurt and disappointment to pass without picking them up and putting them in my bag. We don't choose the illness, the diagnosis, the separation, or the death, but carry them we must. In my bag I quickly but thoughtfully choose my faith, my family and my friends. There is room in my bag for hope and for joy to cushion the fragile, so I take them off the conveyer belt and add them to what is essential. I've decided if I continue to keep my bag mostly full with happy helpful things there will be little space to fill with negative thoughts and actions. It is easier to carry hope rather than bitterness. Stones of hatred are heavier than pebbles of joy. When I was small I was able only to carry small things, as I became bigger and stronger I was able to carry a heavier load. As I approach this later stage in life I need to be more conscious and be smarter and carry only what I need. It's time to forever get rid of unwanted regret, resentment, hurt, failure, and loss.

"He who would travel happily must travel light."
~ Antoine de Saint-Exupery

Choose carefully your fellow traveler. There is much to learn from each other to fine tune our packing choices for both our luggage and our baggage. Experience is sometimes the best teacher. Of utmost importance is to choose someone who is going in the same direction and the same destination.

"The man who goes alone can start today; but he who travels with another must wait till the other is ready."
~ Thoreau

If you once had a very large suitcase, try a somewhat smaller one. If you once needed four pairs of shoes, try two. If you once clung to anger, try not putting it in the bag. If you think you can't part with the anger, put it in a closed, zippered, locked compartment, so it won't infiltrate the rest of the contents. Contain it this time and maybe on the next journey you can take it completely out of the bag.

"All journeys have secret destinations of which the traveler is unaware." ~ Buber

A friend has dubbed these writings my travel journal, and as such I have been planning, packing, repacking. and reevaluating what I'll accept, put in my bag, and take with me. Thanks for choosing to accompany me on this journey. It has made all the difference. It has been more fun, more enjoyable, and easier to bear, and I have learned so much from the sharing. I have stood on your strong shoulders and the view is beautiful, and we have partnered together. Be prepared and always keep your bag and suitcase handy, essentials packed, relationships intact, and then add what you need when you know your destination, and don't forget to choose wisely the people you wish to invite to share the adventure.

"We are often so caught up in our destination that we forget to appreciate the journey, especially the goodness of the people we meet on our way."

~ Anonymous

CHAPTER SEVENTEEN

WHERE HAVE ALL THE THURSDAYS GONE, LONG TIME PASSING

For thirteen Thursdays which began in December, progressed through January, plodded through February, and coasted through nearly half of March it has been Thursdays with Lori, and I coined those words after reading the familiar book, *"Tuesdays with Morrie"*, by Mitch Albom. The book was the result of the writer meeting Morrie on Tuesdays as he chronicled his journey toward death.

For twelve of those days my husband and I were on the road anywhere from 7:00- 8:00 AM depending on my appointment time and the not to be forgotten unpredictable Minnesota weather. The other time a friend picked me up, we stopped for a hot drink and a yummy snack, and then she dropped me off for my weekly treatment. Early on, my man would stay long enough to meet with the raven haired, forty something oncologist and then be on his way to work. I sat in my recliner, received my treatment, and began the process of accepting and establishing my own pathway through a cold and impersonal space. I needed to manage those 4 1/2 -5 hours productively, and over time I changed my own thinking about the landscape of the space.

Change doesn't come easily, and sometimes it is easier to build a wall of indifference as a protection against whatever as one deals with one's own calamity. Only then can one reach beyond the shock or pain into the space of another fellow traveler who is trying to do much the same as we each muddle on. The time at the infusion has always passed quickly with just the process of it all. The day always begins with weighing in, taking the vitals, sterilizing the port area, flushing the port, inserting the special core needle, the blood draws, meeting with the oncologist, waiting for the test results, and finally beginning with the saline solution, premeds of steroids, acid reducer and such to protect the body from the onslaught of the toxic cancer drugs, and ends with the removal of the needle and flushing the port and taking vitals again. During and in between all those procedures there was always time for a snack, and a complimentary lunch that was exactly the same each week, for knitting headbands, writing letters and thank you notes, for reading magazines or a book. In time, I tried slowly and carefully to reach out to the other patients who occupied their own beige faux leather chair on Recliner Row. Basically, that is how the time was spent each week with the roving pharmacist punctuating the space at intervals. The nurses rotated through the patients so they didn't get attached to any single one, were exposed to various treatments and procedures, and patients. I developed my own favorite nurses, and we continued our connections whether I was assigned to them or not.

My pick up limo service consisted of my daughter being there eleven of the thirteen times to collect me and my bags. Then we would do Christmas shopping, lunch, general shopping, hot chocolate breaks, Christmas returns, grocery shopping, and other mundane activities to celebrate another treatment completed. Two other days a long time friend with her shiny, sparkling clean, red Cadillac cruised up to the front door to whisk me away. One day she and I met her daughter who is my goddaughter and her mother-in-law for lunch and on the final #12 treatment just the two of us had a celebration lunch. What a special gift this was for me.

I never dreaded Thursdays, but looked forward to crossing another week off the schedule and spending precious time with special people. My new schedule is an abbreviated treatment every third Thursday for the remainder of the year. Now, I will have to determine a new plan for those intervening Thursdays.

Each patient I have met has had their own schedule and treatment plan. Some like me are there every Thursday, others every third Thursday, and others are on totally different schedules. On my last weekly Thursday, I wanted to make contact with those I have met over the course of 13 weeks. I spoke with the lavender hat young woman and met her husband for the first time and we exchanged names. Her name in Sonia and next week will be her final week of this treatment and then she will begin radiation. I imagine I will never see Sonia again, because that is what happened to the beige hat woman named Carol. With my cold steel infusion pole in hand, I move from recliner to recliner talking briefly with those individuals I have met and Sonia was the first.

I stop at the private room with a bed where Claudia has been every third week on her rotation, so I will probably see her in three weeks. She has short cropped brown hair and is much further along in her treatment. We greet, exchange a few words and I move on.

Recliner Row is a relatively small space and it is impossible to not overhear conversations taking place in other parts of the room. Several weeks ago a new couple arrived and she took chair number 5. Over a three week period I caught tidbits of her conversations and determined she must live in my area. I decided it was time to talk with her and her husband and indeed she was from our town. So for the past few weeks I have walked over to her chair and we have talked. Last week for the first time she waved and called out a greeting when she arrived to occupy her chosen chair. Today, when I returned from meeting with the oncologist, she was in chair number 2 right next to mine. We could carry on our conversation as we sat side by side. People are so interesting. In the 6 weeks never has her husband even looked up to acknowledge me, let alone utter a single word. She has only two more Thursday treatments and then she needs to make a huge decision whether she will attempt a stem cell procedure. She too will be gone when I return in 3 weeks. I am reminded again that friendships are for a reason, a season, or a lifetime and each is important.

I unplug the monitor, grab my steel pole and walk over to chair number 4 and the leather laced fashion boot lady named Diane. Her husband hops up immediately from his chair to offer it to me. We begin, I believe, one of the strangest conversations I've had in my whole life. I have yet to figure out what I should do with the information she shared. For 15-20 minutes she told and retold things and events that left me feeling almost helpless and speechless. I returned to my chair saddened and shocked at what I have learned. What responsibility do I have to share this with people who would have the skill to help her?

I find myself amazed at the crystalline morphing that has taken place in this space I have called Recliner Row in a mere 13 weeks. It is bittersweet. I am excited and relieved that I have advanced to the next stage of my treatment, but I am saddened to know that these people will no longer be a part of my weekly routine. How does one move from seemingly cold indifference to one of familiarity and comfort?

I joke with the nurses as I pack my sturdy overflowing black bag containing my projects, put on my black coat, and march through the double doors to not return for three weeks. It is an ambivalent feeling and I am surprised at the scope of my thoughts, but there is something new to be concerned about. After meeting with the cardiologist earlier this week, he's decided I need to be on a heart medication because my heart is beating too fast. This has caught me off guard. One treatment regimen is finished, and now a totally new chapter begins. For all these weeks the chemotherapy drug has had no effect on my energy level, but two hours after I begin taking the new drugs for the heart, I feel like I have been run over by a Mack truck. My arms and legs feel like lead weights, and the marching and soldiering on that I most often do doesn't seem to work. I am stopped dead in my tracks. Little else has changed, my bags are packed, so I must refocus and regroup and be joyful, thankful, and grateful as I begin this new phase. The unwelcome intruders of disappointment and discouragement must be booted out so there is room for the positive thoughts. The sun still shines, my family and friends are still here, and it's still me, as I sit in a comfortable light beige chair in my family room. I look out the window on the most beautiful spring snowfall as three whitetail deer stand at attention at the base of the marsh with their ears perked , listening for the slightest sound and their eyes searching for the smallest of movement.

A constant stream of new faces with other names will rotate through those familiar faux leather beige chairs on Recliner Row. May they find the space inviting and comforting if not at first in time and may they meet kind and caring people to help them on their way. I will gladly give up my weekly Thursday recliner and settle for every third week for the remainder of the year. I have learned far more than I would have chosen, but have added a new dimension to my relationships. Many people have shared their own struggles and that has enriched both our lives. Other friends began their own journey shortly after I began mine and we have traveled together giving encouragement as best we could.

Literally, my black suitcase and my black backpack are packed with clothes for warm and sunny weather as I embark on a Caribbean cruise. I have carefully considered what to pack and include. In addition to the sundry items of medication, clothing, hats, suntan lotion, and books, I have an ample supply of those other things that help us through or over the rough spots. We are going with family, so we have chosen our traveling companions with great care and consideration, and we look forward to a change of pace and a change of place.

CHAPTER EIGHTEEN

LAUGHABLE MOMENTS

I'm not this funny, laughable, life of the party person. My usual method is wit or dry humor, but I will share what to me were laughable or somewhat laughable moments as I have been on this journey. Give me some grace and leeway as I relate some incidents and experiences in no particular order.

I looked in the mirror this morning to survey the hair crop. Despite the special keep your hair fertilizer (shampoo) I have been using, I have seen no positive effects of said product. Be careful of the outlandish promises noted by those trying to sell the products. There is a sprinkling of 3/8"- 1/2" hair that have remained, but you could count the number of hairs on my head without being God. It has been 3 weeks since the end of the main cancer drug treatment, and I see 1/64" - 1/32" soft white sprigs pushing their way out. Is that measurable? Being a farmer's daughter I'm wondering if there is some sort of government program to help me out. I'm thinking it will be a failed crop for the entire growing season. Where do I sign up for crop failure? I must always count my blessings because for 3-4 months I've had the smoothest legs on the planet with no stubble to mow. Time saved. Happy to say or sad to say whether I see the glass half full or half empty, it is spring and a new crop is making its appearance. The positive farmer that I am, I have high hopes and I don't think the temperature or the rainfall will make any difference. While we are on the subject of hair, I have been pleased that those stray ugly chin and upper lip hairs have gone missing. I like that. I smile.

Hair prosthesis follow-up. I never related the story of the first time I wore my wig in public. We were out with friends, talking, eating, laughing, and moving most facial muscles at some point or another. To begin with I had positioned my wig so that the bangs overlapped my eyebrows and the top of the frame on my rusty red glasses. As the evening went on, the wig crept further up and further up until the bottom of the bangs were way above my eyebrows. I felt it, but how do I discreetly pull the wig down while in public? I decided there is no cool way, just do it. What I learned was catch it before it goes too far. I laugh.

Briefly I told you about my initial experience of trying on and purchasing at Underneath It All when I was being fitted for my prosthesis for that very first time. I went home with my precious prosthesis and three new bras in this darling medium sized pink bag. The next day it is time to put the merchandise to use. I'm getting dressed and I put on my new garb and a sumptuous deep red cashmere sweater and take a look at myself in the huge bathroom mirror in front of me. What? For all these years I've have a matched set, but not now. Take it off, put it back in the cute pink bag, get dressed, back in the car, and march back to the shop and declare, "This just won't do". Kathy, the owner, sends me to the dressing room to put it on again so she can take a look. She looks at me, smiles and says she thinks I am right, but I'm the first person who has ever wanted to be smaller. So smaller it is, I like it that way. It's familiar and comfortable. I smile.

I am at the doctor's office and now I am told to get on the scale to weigh in. Do you ever take off your shoes? I do, and now I'm thinking this prosthesis weighs as much as my shoe. Oh the warped mind. I laugh to myself.

There are those days when I just have to add a little humor in the everyday situations. With all the appointments, tests, surgeries, and weekly infusion, I was so tired of being asked my name, my birthdate, whether I had fallen, or was I safe in my own home. Actually irritated is probably a more accurate word to describe my feeling. I asked my daughter to print me a card with all the answers to those questions and laminate it. She did a fabulous job making it pretty too and I have punched a hole in it, and added a colorful lanyard. Whenever I check in at urgent care, the clinic, the hospital, and Recliner Row I just pull out my card, present it for them to read and I don't have to answer those questions any more. More people have chuckled, laughed out loud, made comments, changed their attitudes, and connected with me in a personal way more than any other single thing I have done. People laughed and I smiled.

People do and say the dumbest things. OK, so I've just exposed myself. I am totally naked, they have looked, prodded, pushed, pulled and probed the most private parts of your body and now the examination is finished complete over. What do they say, "I'll step out of the room so you can get dressed". Like I need privacy now? This makes me smile.

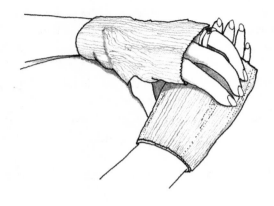

I walked into the pharmacy today where my daughter works to pick up my RX. I'd tried especially hard to look sharp with my Rachel Welch wig, and my new red fingerless gloves because I am off to meet a friend for lunch. One of the pharmacists calls out, "Those are really sexy gloves". My first thought and then reply was "That's pretty scary for someone my age". Maybe there is still hope for me. It made me smile.

Earlier I talked about choosing carefully a traveling companion and the benefits that are derived from doing just that. The same principle can be used for choosing a life partner, and I've decided I made a very good choice. He has made some funny statements when I have been a bit too serious, which I might say isn't very often. A few months back when I was doing some research online about a prosthesis, I was totally shocked and amazed at the cost of the simple device and said it was utterly ridiculous. He just casually says, "Try Craig's list". I had to laugh out loud.

I smile when I remember the incident when I was having one of the many tests. The nurse in charge had begun the usual questions and instead of answering them I just held up my laminated name card. She continued with her task and looks at me and says, "Do you lip read"? She thought I was deaf. I was a little embarrassed for myself and her.

Someone sent me this crazy looking cat card and it made me laugh. At the same time several people kept asking what my hair looked like. It was growing out and since I wasn't going to send a picture of myself, I sent this picture of the cat. I wrote, "You wanted to know what my hair looks like under my wig. Here it is. I am sorry I was such a sour pus the day the picture was taken." No more suspense.

CHAPTER NINETEEN

PAPER ANGELS

The sleek black Honda cruises down the tree lined street, and turns slowly into the concrete pavers driveway. The Genie garage door opener is pushed and the cream colored door makes its way gradually but confidently on the metal tracks and disappears into the rafters. The car with its two occupants glides into its assigned place. As the door begins its descent and lumbers closed, the woman passenger yanks the wig off her tender head, because she can stand the constant pressure not one second more. The driver smiles, this is nothing new, it has happened before, it will happen again, because the constant pressure is relentless. The head breathes and a sigh of relief floods the car. We are home.

My writing started with a spark of an idea when sleep eluded, became a commitment, and continues although less frequently. Noticeably, something began to change within me and between us. By our shared experience it has changed who we are and our relationships with each other whether relative, friend, or stranger. For many of us our friendships have deepened as we have delved into the very core of our beings and have thought and many times shared on a totally different level being vulnerable to each other and our inner selves. I've faced my mortality, the importance of our relationship, the impact we have on each other and in some cases the details of it all are just too much to bear. Some have pulled away, and I understand and appreciate the importance of that also. We are different people and we need each to be true to ourselves.

Everywhere on farms or small towns, large cities or country side, by the lake or near the mountains, on street corners or sidewalks, on busy streets and back roads, we are forced to face a new reality. Your enthusiasm for my sharing has sparked and fueled new thoughts. I am humbled by your confidence and encouragement, but am assured that this path was one I needed, not wanted to take. To open our eyes and hearts to others, to be available to each other, to be used, to be buoyed up by collective enthusiasm, sometimes fearful and trembling to complete the circle makes the journey bearable, exciting, and questioning at times. Whether I say the wrong words, shy away, or make other mistakes, we must march forward crumpling and discarding our mistakes and imperfections like used paper into a nearby waste basket so that along the way we become more the person we want and care to be. It matters only that we take a chance to begin anew with a blank sheet of paper before us and strive to be a paper angel floating in and out of the lives of relatives, friends and strangers leaving them changed, better off, or encouraged because of our visit. In the writing process I've put chosen words to paper, rejected other words, embellished still other thoughts, and then decided the thought complete. Then and only then is the working draft crumpled and discarded.

This week I face another day at Recliner Row with its workers and patients. From the time I arrive until the time I leave there is only one familiar face in the occupied beige faux leather chairs, but there are many recognizable nurses and workers.

It is spring and the leather lace fashion boot woman has discarded her winter boots, and makes her bouncy entrance in tight fitting skinny jeans and wears nondescript ballet flats. She is thin, tiny, and wears a visor rather than a hat because her hair has grown to a length able to make a statement on its own. The people we meet are fighting battles we know nothing about, so be kind, and kind again. I will be a simple paper angel to her.

I have found it more difficult to connect with people on the three week schedule. Today, I have this little burst of inspiration and nudging to reach out again to find a face that will become familiar in our shared space in Recliner Row. It would be much easier to close myself off in my own little world and read a book or write a note, but I believe I can make a difference. Lives are knitted and threaded together for a reason and a purpose.

Spring has come with new life, bursts of plant growth, blooming tulips, blossoming trees, and lush green grass, so in that thinking I need to begin anew.

Summer will likewise parade before us with days at the lake, afternoons at the beach, picnics in the park, lunch on the patio, walks on the trails, rides in the country, visits from family and friends, more garden blooms to enjoy and so too will my treatment continue and so Celebrate Life.

Fall will descend upon us before we are ready, the leaves will turn their brilliant hues and lazily float to the earth, the days will be bright and crisp, a cozy wool sweater will feel good again, the apples red on sturdy branches hang, the corn will be golden brown, the leaves will rustle as we walk, and the treatment will continue and so Celebrate Life.

Winter approaches with thoughts of holiday festivities, warm and cozy fires, snuggling together for warmth, sipping a hot drink with friends, and an end to my treatment. I will Celebrate Life. I do not wish away any of the coming days, weeks, months, or moments. Each are but a fleeting moment to be enjoyed, to be cherished, to be lived, and to be shared. Your enthusiasm has given me wings to fly. I have been infused with an ever grateful heart, your thoughtfulness has overwhelmed me, your patience has touched me, your presence has comforted me, your love has softened me. All of these have been monumental in the journey to Celebrate Life. I will be a living breathing paper angel attempting to brush lives I encounter, floating unaware at times, leaving a smile or a hug in my wake, and looking for that special person I can touch.

I remember all those stories I carried home with me after a day on Recliner Row to share with you. I think about the beige crocheted hat woman, the fiery redhead, the lavender colored hat woman, and the woman from my town. The names will fade and some have faded, but the faces remain and their stories have left an incredible impact on my life. These woman have passed in front of me and have left their lasting reflections and have altered the way I see seemingly random people placed daily in my life. I think I can strive to be a simple, plain, ministering spirit paper angel. With a cloudburst of paper angels we could change the world in which we live.

CHAPTER TWENTY

FLYING FLOATING PAPER ANGELS

Paper angels are like paper dolls. They come in all shapes and sizes, young and old alike, all colors and nationalities, and of different genders. They travel easily because they are flat, weigh little, and they can fly. Let me tell you about a few flying floating angels I have met during this journey. They are easily recognizable by me and perhaps by you.

It is on a cold winter Saturday morning with the ground blanketed with white snow, and the house is toasty warm when the phone rings. I answer it, and it takes me a few seconds to grasp the name and connect the dots from the past to the here and now. It is a call from a fellow in Virginia, a guy I dated in high school and college, and a man I had seen only once or twice in the last fifty years. Somehow he tracked down my phone number and took the time to call. We spent the better part of an hour or more talking about our lives, sharing stories about our families, where we lived, what was important to us, and reconnecting in ways totally unimaginable. He shared his own pain in losing a twin sister to breast cancer. We have that common thread that manifests itself in the tapestry of our lives. On that cold day there was warmth, a smile, and laughter that filled the house as we bonded again after all these years. He was my paper angel that day clad in a boyish shy smile, a bit bashful still, but always kind, friendly, and caring as I remembered him so many years ago.

A dear friend offered to fly here from Colorado to be with me. Although I declined having her come, I was touched by her offer and sent her the warm blanket story to attempt to have her understand. When her son and daughter-in-law were traveling she asked them to bring back a hat for me. What a darling navy hat they chose purchased in Scotland.

Though paper angels are flat and sometimes fragile, this single angel came bearing homemade soup not once, not twice, but many times. It was not just the soup, but she settled in that comfortable beige club chair in our family room with limber feet tucked under her body, talking, and sharing the beautiful woman story. Her hands misshapen by arthritis and particularly painful that day found comfort as I heated up my cherry pit pack and placed it in her hands. She could feel the heat and it dulled the pain in her aching joints. It soothed our souls as we laid bare our busy lives each open to a mutual give and take that has forever nourished our friendship over many years. Weeks before she shared the 10 beautiful swans story from her lake cabin, so that I could savor the beauty of the imagined scene. I am reminded of another time when I was feeling a bit low she told me to pick up My Big Girl Pants and put them on. It brought laughter to that day. How I have needed that thought over the past few months keeping the big girl pants mended and close at hand.

Another call came from a male cousin who said he didn't write letters, he didn't e-mail and he rarely made a phone call. He wanted me to know he was thinking of me and wished me the best. He cared to take the time.

A married couple we often go to movies with and out to dinner purchased a PBS series, "Downton Abbey". They knew we were spending most of our time at home and thought we might enjoy the English series. What fun it was to curl up by the warm cozy fire and watch.

Most weeks the coffee shop angel and I have met in one of the local area coffee shops, whether it is in Wayzata or Minnetonka with their coveted brown leather chairs neatly pulled up next to the cozy warm fireplace, or Excelsior and Deephaven. We sip, she green tea, and hot chocolate for me as we walk this journey hand in hand and side by side. We laugh and sometimes cry, unable to squelch the tears that hover so close to the surface. We reach into each others lives of collected stories, incidents, and shared family legacy, that has so tightly knit our relationship together with a commonness that binds. Almost weekly for more than a year she has been my coffee shop angel.

Many years ago we lived in Canada. While there I met this wonderful lady when we worked together to develop a children's church ministry at our church. We became great friends and have maintained our friendship over the years. She lives in British Columbia and calls often to check on me as I did her when she lost her husband. She's my Canadian paper angel.

My husband's former boss called often and e-mailed me notes of encouragement and sent articles he thought I might enjoy. He'd had his own battle with cancer and he understood. Excerpts from one of his notes: "Cancer can be the beginning of a new and wonderful part of your life. This has happened for me", "You and I still have time to live, to love, to travel, to experience many wonderful things, to teach, to give and importantly , to get ourselves and our loved ones ready for anything", "So live....Live your life now, and tomorrow. Fight your disease as best you can, but concentrate all the while on how fortunate you have been in your life, and how fortunate you are now to be alive, and to be able to remember so many wonderful experiences. Then always keep in mind that you now have the chance to live even more life, but now with a unique and sharper focus on the opportunity you have been given to create a final chapter of wonderful experiences."

Although I don't speak French, I do have a French paper angel. She among all those English speaking paper angels has flooded my mailbox with encouraging e-mails, letters, and cards. Lucky for me she speaks my language. Distance need not separate us.

A developer my husband has worked with for years and has weathered his own bout with cancer sent Cadbury chocolate almond candy bars for me. He'd say, "Take this to your bride". A Cadbury paper angel.

There is another soup angel, but this one sports a cowboy hat and wears trousers as he delivers his fabulous soup. I appreciate his culinary skills. He may be quiet and walk softly, but he carries a big stick, and he has mastered the cooking and the caring. He is married to the local book paper angel who has been a lending library to me. There are no late fees or set time to return the books. There is no hounding to hurry up and finish. I have walked away from their home with two shopping bags loaded with books to stack in my wardrobe ready and waiting to give pleasure upon reading.

These have been a few of the paper angels floating and flying in my life, touching me in profound ways and making the journey so much easier and enjoyable.

I am ready for a journey of another kind and it is two weeks until our ambitious vacation departure to Europe. I feel fairly well organized with most of the hotel reservations complete, car rental arranged, and possible clothing items hanging in the guest room patiently waiting to be folded and tucked away neatly in the black Eagle Creek carry on luggage. Three new books are stacked in an orderly pile next to the carry on, pills counted and deposited in their Sunday to Saturday plastic pill box, an Ace knee support lays close at hand in case it is needed, the travel journal purchased and ready to record the intimate details of the much anticipated adventure, a blunt nose fingernail scissors to cut out pictures from brochures, a box of 2 sided photo stickers to mount them, the list goes on with all the thinking and planning purposeful.

Next week I will pick up Euros at the bank, sign up for texting on my phone, cancel mail delivery, and fine tune every minuscule detail that remains, but today I will venture out into the shopping world to look for a cute new frock to add to my well worn travel clothes. I am dressed early and donned my trusty wig. On previous outings I had wished I had taken a turban hat with me in case the wig was uncomfortable so into my LeSportsac bag my turban goes and I hurry to the car. Less than 5 miles down the road with one hand on the steering wheel I yanked off my wig and nylon sock liner that so tightly clung to my head and tugged on the white turban. What a pleasure.

I arrived at Macy's and skirted one department after another exploring the possibilities. With no fun loving frock calling to me I went to the Galleria to continue my search. There I was poking around, looking to find the perfect thing I was willing to shell out the money for, two young woman maybe late 30's or early 40's walked boldly up to me and one said, "What a cute hat, where did you get it?" This is definitely strange because the hat is a nondescript white turban on which I sewed fake hair. I admitted quickly that I had lost my hair during cancer treatment, and I told them I had purchased it at It's Still Me. With a quiet soft, tentative voice the younger of the two said she was beginning chemo on Monday and was having a port installed later this week. Thus began a 15-20 minute conversation where I shared my experience and encouraged her in hers. I asked her for her name and told her I would pray for her. She lives in the same town as do I and beginning Monday she will sit in one of the beige faux leather chairs at Recliner Row. Who could orchestrate this meeting? They were overwhelmed with thankfulness, and as they turned to walk away the older sister put her arm around her sister comforting her and said, "There are no chance encounters". As I left the store and I hurried to my black Honda I was dodging the raindrops. I wasn't there for shopping but appointed to be Maxine's paper angel.

Maxine lives a mere 5-7 miles down the road from me, but I have no idea where. That short distance is separated by roads and driveways, stores and houses, grass and trees, mailboxes and fence posts. I will find her but that is a story for later. I may have come home empty handed from shopping, but my heart was full and overflowing.

I made my way to the church on 101 in Wayzata to celebrate the life of another. The rain clouds vanished and it turned into a sun drenched day. I sat quietly in the familiar pew of our former church to pay my respect to a woman whose journey much like mine began 10 years ago and ended far too abruptly for her and her family. The comforting words of the minister, the beautiful voice singing "On Eagles Wings", and the reciting and reading of familiar scriptures brings a quiet peace to my soul. It is good, it is right, and it is necessary to gather together in solidarity to demonstrate to the family the value of her life to each one of us who sit frozen in our places with our own individual thoughts and needs.

Later, words of condolences, words of comfort, long kept memories shared, words of promise, and hugs of support become the hallmark of my conversation with her husband and her three sons. To share with the family and to share with each other lends credence to the long held ritual and smacks of reality in my own life. There is a joy, comfort, and hope that permeates my whole being and it is good. With my fashionable (words of someone else) taupe corduroy hat with fake hair as a shield against a quick recognition of the cancer patient, with a smooth black down knee length coat to protect from the cold, and my husband by my side, I walk away from this church, this memorial, touched, changed, and sobered by the realness of it all. A paper angel I can be.

I take my pure white paper, fold it accurately, and with scissors in hand cut carefully. What do I see but a row of cookie cutter paper angels laid out across my desk? Although the paper angels don't have faces of their own, I imprint a face on them as I am reminded of a kindness, a goodness, an encouragement bestowed upon me. I feel the flutter of the angel wings as they float and fly in and out of my life.

I have heard the knocking, felt the tapping, experienced the fluttering, and seen the results of paper angels floating and flying. Snatch them if you can, enjoy them and send them on their way. Come fly with me.

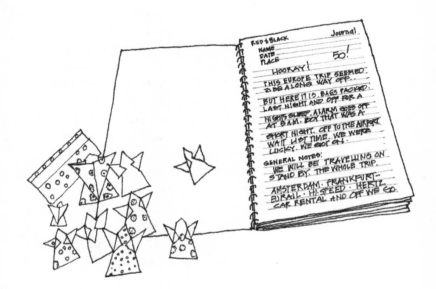

CHAPTER TWENTY-ONE

COME FLY WITH ME
LITTLE PAPER ANGELS

It was my every intention that "Flying, Floating Paper Angels" would probably be my last segment, but as circumstance would have it, people call, people e-mail, and people encouraged me to write more, because they wonder and are concerned when too much time passes and they have heard nothing.

A few days before embarking on our 50th anniversary trip to Europe and after wondering whether such an ambitious trip was feasible, I remember my much repeated advice to my 90 something mother. She often said she was too old or couldn't walk very far, and therefore she was going to stay home. I always told her that you can see a lot from the car window, so don't miss an opportunity. I've decided to take my own advice after carefully considering the luggage to take, and leaving behind any negative baggage. Being packed and ready to go, I waited for the day of departure to arrive.

A thick puffy white envelope arrived at the house. Upon opening a Host Of Angels spilled out in front of me and on to my lap. My friend, who spends summers in Oregon, was relating my journey and the paper angel story while she was walking with a buddy of hers. The story of our connectedness although miles separate us rang true. So my sharing led to her sharing. My friend lovingly requested her friend to try to make colorful folded paper origami angels so she might send them to me as an encouragement . Although her friend had never done angels before, she tried, she succeeded, they were perfect and beautiful. I smiled, felt the constriction in my throat, and a warmth of caring filled my body, and I knew the journey is worthwhile. Reach out, touch, reach out, touch, reach out, the circle continues. Behold many colored, many patterned, many sized angels lay before me, and I knew instantly that one of those paper angels would accompany me on our trip. The angels came in three sizes and I chose the smallest angel adorned in a sunny stunning yellow print with tiny white flowers and bright green leaves. I tucked her carefully away inside our red spiraled black cover trip journal. She was thin, light weight and she was the last item I packed, a colorful memento of my special friend, a reminder to me of my role to be a paper angel myself whenever possible. The three of us set off, the groom and bride of 50 years with silver in our hair or lack thereof, and the precious angel just days old. We embarked without informing the littlest angel of the adventure ahead.

Another friend, who previously worked for the airlines shared her buddy passes with us and thus we were traveling standby. With little difficulty we left Minneapolis very early in the morning on a sunny, fluffy cloud filled day, and happily arrived in Detroit to await the most difficult part of the journey which is to secure a seat on the flight over the water. We have a short layover and we are listed to fly from Detroit to Frankfurt. As the regular paying reservation passengers continue to board, names are called from the stand by list. Finally, our friends are called, and they board the flight. There are no more available seats, the door of the plane shuts with finality. We are left standing with 10 other people in the same predicament. I make a quick call with a quivering voice to our friends on the plane to tell them we didn't make it, and not to worry we'd figure something out.

The littlest angel has no clue (nor do we) what lies ahead, and how often she will be called upon. I have no idea if angels are gender specific, but I have chosen to refer to my angel in the feminine because we must travel so closely together, in intimate settings and it makes me more comfortable when she is called upon to pave the way as I finger the tips of her tiny wings. We did get on board the next plane, but the destination was Amsterdam, a far cry from Frankfurt where we are to pick up our rental car. Each time we waited in line the same people waited with us. The three guys on the list ahead of us and the two of us were scrambling to figure out how we would get from Amsterdam to Frankfurt when we landed. Planes, Trains, or Automobiles? Two of the three guys were savvy computer guys, who checked flights and costs of planes and trains and rental cars. When we landed one of the fellows, a guy fittingly named Michael, was waiting for us as we existed the gangway with all the information we needed to make our choice, he his choice, and the other two decided they were in no hurry so off to the bar they went. These were all Americans and we all spoke the same language, so it was relatively easy. The littlest angel who had been taken from the Host of Angel was able to ather around her and us other paper angels to help us on our way. How would she and we fare when we went from foreign country to foreign country? Would she be able to speak the foreign paper angel languages?

This was just the beginning of an incredible journey where the littlest angel never ceased to amaze us. I wished I had had a pocket full of paper angels to leave one with each of the people who befriended us on our path, but I only had the words, "You are our angel today". Even those words evoked smiles and acceptance of their new status with comical utterances. When we walk in our world we need to watch and observe carefully, look into the eyes of people, discern a willingness, check their demeanor to determine whom you might find as your paper angel or whom you might be a paper angel to give of yourself. I found it was imperative to keep the littlest angel close at hand. With little time to spare we hurried to the counter, bought our train tickets, boarded the train, and we were on our way hopefully ready and prepared for the road ahead. The train speeds on, the seamless rails make for a smooth ride, the view from the train window is lovely and so we settle back and relax as we move toward our destination. We arrive, it has taken most of the day. We scurry to find a room for the night and we are back on track.

Early the next morning we arrive at the car rental, take our turn at the counter, and proceed to the parking garage to retrieve our car. The stout German woman inspector walks around the car and makes Xs on her car diagram of the nicks and dings, half absent side mirror, loose bumper, and holes in the floor mats. We put the key in the ignition and turn on the car. The engine sounds terrible and the lights don't work. She asks, "How long will you rent the car?" Two weeks I answer, "TWO WEEKS" this will never do. She pockets the key so they can't rent it to someone else and we make our way back to the counter to start again. An angel watches over us.

Once in the next car Rothenberg on the Tauber beckons us again with its walled city, quaint buildings, secluded gardens,

favorite hotel and German restaurant, ornate and interesting shop signs, and flowers spilling and cascading from pots, window boxes and huge street planters. We spend a couple of days here to soak up the pleasant atmosphere, relax, and find comfort in the familiar.

We continue our journey as we drive to pick up our friends at Romrod Castle. The four of us, 50th anniversary celebrants are together again as we hopscotch from country to country together for a few days. We are intrigued with the new, an outdoor concert in Maastricht, Netherlands with pageantry and fireworks. Then we are on to Brugge, Belgium a remarkably preserved and a wonderfully beautiful city. We have a chance to walk the narrow streets, sneak into a pub for dinner, and find time to observe the locals.

We cruised down its many canals and surveyed the wonderful mix of architectural styles and almost rubbed shoulders with the beautiful white swans parading and preening themselves

on white feather strewn trampled grass. I am reminded of my 10 beautiful trumpeter swan friend back in Minnesota. The view from the boat is breathtaking. With joy, thankfulness, and gratefulness I cherish the thoughts and hug the memories close. Then we are on to Brussels where we parted with our friends as they went home and we proceeded on our own.

Long before we set foot on foreign soil, we planned our trip with the aim to include a few favorite places, but mostly to explore new and different places. Checking with the travel guru, Rick Steves, when looking for a small quaint village on the eastern edge of France I chose an out of the way place, Eguisheim. The drive was long, and we knew approximately where it was but around and around we went, stopping here and there, asking old and young alike, but the language barrier was indeed present and overwhelming. Standing on a corner with people and cars passing, with map in hand, town name written on a piece of paper we approached one person after another, but for some the language barrier was too much and they just passed on. Finally, a tall slender, good looking French speaking young man accompanied by his chestnut brown haired very pregnant wife paused long enough to understand our predicament. He tried to talk, but with no comprehension on our part he switched to arm movements and gestured for us to get in our car and follow them in their automobile. We snaked through little villages and wide open countryside and abruptly he pulls over, stops, and points to the name of our town on the sign. We all get out and a handshake for the guys and a hug for the gals, and we get in our vehicles. We mouthed a thank you, nodded our heads, and tooted our horn in salute to another angel willing to assist a lost traveler. The journey was worth the hassle as we embraced the vineyards nestled in the cradle of the Alsace region.

Eguisheim, the small medieval village with narrow, concentric streets, half-timbered houses, flowers bubbling from planters, ancient fountains, and most surprising of all storks nesting high atop buildings and churches putting on a fabulous display of parenting for our pleasure and enjoyment. The littlest angel tucks her feet under her pretty printed party dress, puts her arms and hands behind her head, leans back and delights in the loveliest of days of rest, wine and roses.

We steadily move forward marking off the days, the places, and the reservations on our itinerary. A long day of driving awaits and we are cruising along the highway being passed by fast moving fancy cars, enjoying the view from the car window, loving the sunshine, the villages, and the clouds when before us appears a sensational rainbow totally enveloped in a single wispy cloud. The rainbow cloud follows us as we twist and turn mile after mile on our way to enchanted Bellagio, Italy. We arrive and our angel basks in the warm sunshiny day as she sits by Lake Como surrounded by a chain of mountains, visits Villa Melzi Gardens with its rare and exotic plants, ancient trees, monuments and marble statues, and walks the steep narrow streets.

A new day arrives and we must continue on. We check out of our hotel, we drive to the ferry, pay our money, board the ferry and we experience the pleasure of the panorama. At the hotel we have asked directions and we are confident once we are off the ferry it will be easy. So begins another adventure, up, up, up we go, hairpins, winding up and up. I keep saying stop, pull over look at the view it is spectacular, but we keep going up. Finally, we see this short in stature elderly couple trudging slowly down the incline. We stopped, they stopped, they don't speak English, but they can read the name of the town we have written on a piece of paper. More foreign speaking, LOUDER and slower, it makes no difference. Now it is back to the universally recognized arm waving again for us to turn our car around and go back down the long and winding road. Angels sometimes stroll slowly with a walking stick in hand, wear less than fashionable clothing, dress with sensible shoes, speak a different language, and are difficult to recognize, but they are angels none the less.

Miles and miles later it will take one more older gentleman who speaks English. He tells us to buy a better more detailed map of Austria, then he gets in his car, and leads us miles down unknown roads to deposit us on a known highway that will lead us to the tunnel and Hallstatt, Austria. With a wave of his arm, he turns and returns to where he has come. It has been 11 hours since we boarded the ferry in Bellagio on a rather ambitious day trip. Halstatt is a unique village, much more than just beautiful decorative buildings and houses, and a crystal clear Swan Lake with swans gracefully gliding and skimming the surface of the placid water. It has been our fortune to book the honeymoon suite, situated right on the smooth waters surrounded by mountains. What could be more perfect for the bride and groom of 50 years, and the littlest angel rests peacefully, because it has been a long tiring day for all of them?

It is Sunday morning and I am out for a walk and as I

approach the little church nestled in the center of town I hear organ music playing. With little thought I step inside the quaint church, stand at the back for a few minutes, and decide to sit down. I can't understand a word of what is being said, but one can worship even so. In time, the sermon is over and the priest stands in the center, he beckons for the people to come forward and they do forming a semi-circle. He begins the communion ritual. Gathered at the altar are twenty plus local people some dressed in lederhosen, others in church dress finery, and I am the only person sitting silently at the back of the small church.

I decide I am going to participate and partake. As I walk forward he begins passing out the bread, and two people seeing me approach, separate to make room for me in the circle. He gives everyone the bread, blesses it, and moves on to the cup. After I have eaten the bread, I have noticed some have taken the bread and eaten it, and others have kept it. Next comes the communion cup; oh no, it is communal, those who have eaten drink from cup, those who have kept their bread dip into the cup . This is a totally new experience for me; he wipes the cup with a white cloth, and I drink the wine from it, and he goes on to the woman next to me. The priest now goes back around the circle and blesses each person as we all hold hands and sing. Was this listed on my itinerary? The littlest angel knows and smiles.

Angel encounters continued, and memories are gathered, garnered, and cherished. In retrospect there was no need for concern; the path was not always smooth, the road was sometimes long, bumpy, and steep, the energy, strength, vigor, and enthusiasm was in abundance, the views were spectacular, the food sumptuous, the shopping splendid, the towns impressive, the companionship superb, the people we met along the way were admirable, and we have gone the distance.

It is the scheduled day of departure. Notice I said scheduled day, but remember we have no tickets. It is Munich, a different city, but the results are the same. It is the only flight of the day to depart for the States. The passengers with tickets board, names are called for standby and again we are left waiting when the last name is called and the doors are closed. The flight for tomorrow is over booked by way too many and we decide we must go to Amsterdam where there will be at least 19 flights leaving for the States each day. We must get from the airport back to the train station because we have decided we will get to Amsterdam by train. We are standing with that lost look in our eyes trying to figure out where to buy a ticket for the Metro when a gypsy looking lady with a boyish haircut and with a huge dark green backpack approaches us and asks us if we need help. Long story short, she has a group ticket. We pay half the regular price and hurry aboard with her and another cute young woman she has assisted. The young gal that was traveling in our group looks up the schedules and prices of the trains to Amsterdam on her Smart Phone and passes the information on to us. There is little time to catch the next train and, when we get off, the gypsy lady takes us to the machine to buy tickets because if you go to the ticket counter you have to pay an extra fee. The machine won't take my Visa card, so I bolt over to the money machine to get cash.

With minutes to spare and the gypsy lady throwing in a few coins we get our tickets, and we race to the train. It will take the littlest angel and a Host Of Angels to get us all the way home to Minneapolis. It has been a spectacular trip, that was much needed in the midst of my treatment. Any worries are long banished and it was a new focus for both of us. Our daughter is waiting for us when we arrive in Minneapolis and I am whisked to my treatment on Recliner Row.

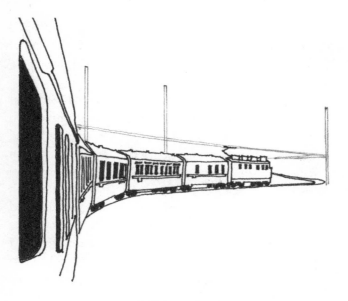

EPILOGUE

It has been in excess of five years since my diagnosis. I have had no major problems and the prognosis is great. I continue my regular visits with the oncologist. The need for these visits has been extended to once a year and I take my daily hormone blocker. Some physical reminders still remain after all these years. During my treatment many of my toenails fell off and it took over a year for them to grow back and a couple of them fell off the second time. One big toenail will never be the same since the nail bed mostly died in the process. My only other residual is aching shins which I hope will go away once I discontinue the hormone blocker. It seems like a small price to pay. I am reminded daily of my mastectomy as I look in the mirror. I didn't choose to have reconstruction surgery, so I usually wear button up blouses or crew neck t-shirts. I have stitched beautiful lace on the tank tops to raise the neckline and to make me feel more comfortable and have added special lace to all my bras. This is a new normal for my life and no matter, I am grateful, thankful and I am joyful.

The phone often rings when people are faced with their own diagnosis or a friend of theirs faces the unknown. I have been able to share with them. I located Maxine and we have continued our relationship and she is doing well. The leather laced boot lady I have met and she is cancer free. I talk to the woman from my home town and her cancer is back and so she continues with treatment. My "Ten Trumpeter Swan" and "Put on your Big Girl Pants" friend was diagnosed with soft tissue sarcoma cancer on her forearm. She credits vanity for the discovery, because she didn't like the appearance of the bump on her arm. After surgery she sat in the same chair as before in my family room and she asked me to make some arm covers. To use the skill I possessed to help gave me a warm feeling and an opportunity to show her I cared. She is doing great.

The littlest angel, her frock not quite so crisp and smooth has traveled often over the past years, tucked away in another black spiral travel journal. She is quite the seasoned traveler and assumes her role easily. She returns home each time and nestles herself back a bit wrinkled in the packet with the host of angels readying herself for yet another journey when she is called upon and needed. The cancer has not stopped us from traveling, but propelled us to do even more and the littlest angel is there to guide the way.

Today, nine drab beige colored faux leather recliners known to me as "Recliner Row" continue to welcome new and old patients. My outstretched hand has welcomed you along this journey with me. Am I the same person I was when I started? Definitely not. Am I glad I have walked this journey? Yes, most definitely. Have I been whittled to the core? Yes. Have I come to more appreciate the love and acceptance of family and friends? Yes. Have I learned to never, never give up? Yes. Do I think I have more to learn? Yes. Is cancer my friend? No way, but it has brought me closer to becoming the person I want to be.

Thanks and more thanks is never enough for all the people who have made my journey easier, brighter, and softer. You have encouraged me and walked with me. You know who you are: family, friends, doctors, nurses, acquaintances, publisher, copy editor, tech man, my husband the sketch master, and more. . . *I am grateful*.